Confessions of a Female Private Investigator

TIFFANY BOND

kisspublications.com.au

Confessions of a Female Private Investigator
First published in Australia by Kiss Publications

© Copyright Tiffany Bond 2009

All rights reserved. No part of this publication may be reproduced, stored in a retrieval system, or transmitted in any form, or by any means, without the prior written permission of the copyright owner. Enquiries should be made to info@kisspublications.com.au

National Library of Australia Cataloguing-in-Publication entry

Bond, Tiffany Faith, 1974 –
Confessions of a Female Private Investigator
ISBN: 978-0-646-51783-4

Cover design and photography by Kevin and Katrina Spark
Edited by Michael Collins
Printed by Fontaine Press Pty Ltd
Cover photo by Katrina Spark

The text for this publication is printed on Envi Carbon Neutral Paper.

Dedication

For my two beautiful girls

Contents

Acknowledgements	ix
About Tiffany Bond	xi
Introduction	xii
A Personal Discovery	1
A Regular Doctor's Appointment	12
The Colour Purple	19
A Hands on Approach	30
Under the Microscope	35
Revenge	44
Fatal Car Accident	50
The Bare Facts	53
Secrets and Lies	63
Sex on Tap	68
Undercover Prostitute	77
Say Cheese	83
The Honey Trap	94
Close Call	105

Playing Fair	111
A Double Life	117
Is Death a Permanent State?	125
Nappy Rash	129
Dark Shadows in Cyber Space	137
Lucky Break	147
It Takes Two to Tango	152
Indecent Assault	158
The Boss from Hell	162
Better Than the Real Thing	173
Smash and Grab	180
Tools of the Trade	183
Investigation Enquiries	194
Our Recommended Businesses	195

Acknowledgements

I would like to sincerely and dearly thank the following people:

Brighid P for her amazing friendship, compassion, support and all the awesome times we've shared; Jason S for his kind assistance; Jim P for all the entertaining stories; Greg E for his encouragement and kind assistance; Lynne B for her enthusiasm and ability to make me laugh; Chris A for her unwavering friendship and support; Mark B for his amazing accounting and always making time for me; Catherine B for her supporting accounting and always having time for a coffee; Kim, Angela, Melanie, Charlene, Gray, Mardi and Selina for all the incredibly great times we've shared; Louise VR for all your amazing support, laughter and champagne; Maggie H and Mark H for their fun times; Monica C for all her stories which always leave me in stitches of laughter; Ron J for his friendship and fantastic handyman work; Jordan C for his friendship, support and laughter; Katrina S for her special friendship, her ability to let me be myself, and her great photography; Kevin S for his friendship, the fact that he always has a great story to tell, and his wonderful graphic design work; Michael H for everything including the IT work, graphics and late night emails; Michael R who believed in me from the beginning; Michael C who supported me throughout this book writing; Rebecca P for her amazingly consistent support and friendship; my two beautiful daughters for bringing beauty and inspiration into my life; my ex-husband, whose actions subsequently fuelled my success and happiness; and my ex-rental agency for evicting me and my daughters, inspiring me to buy the house I now call home.

I'd like to thank my amazing staff, and investigative agents, for helping and supporting me. Detection Group wouldn't be what it is today without them.

I'd also like to thank all my wonderful and admirable clients who have trusted me with their stories and allowed me to help them – I am truly honoured.

About Tiffany Bond

Tiffany Bond is CEO of Detection Group Pty Ltd, a nationwide private investigation firm specialising in infidelity.

She graduated Dux of the Queensland Police Academy in 1997. Her three and a half year police service included almost twelve months undercover duty in the Prostitution Unit in Fortitude Valley, Queensland.

Prior to her police work, Tiffany clocked up three years in debt collection before the age of 21, followed by a career in security at Brisbane Airport, Brisbane's Convention & Exhibition Centre and Southbank.

Tiffany lives in Brisbane with her two daughters.

Introduction

Stories, memories, and experiences can linger with us or fade over the years. Some are meant to be enjoyed, some give us healing, some slip away unexamined, and some are best forgotten. It's the stories that taught me something along the way that I'd like to share, stories that put me on the path I'm on today and made me the person I am.

I shed many tears as this book came together, some of sadness and many of joy. Re-living parts of my life was difficult, and coming to terms with some aspects was even harder. But it was worth it. I was able to experience closure, something I've not allowed myself to do until now.

I hope that my stories will touch you, the reader. While I'm sure that some areas of private investigation will delight and intrigue you, others will certainly shock. And a few readers will think very hard about their own relationships.

If, through this book, I can help any one person understand that they're not alone in their suffering, I have achieved what I set out to do. If these stories put hope into someone's life,

I have achieved what I set out to do. If this book makes someone think twice about betrayal, or supports them in leaving a relationship that is overwhelmingly bad, or encourages them to seek help, then I have achieved what I set out to do.

The private investigation stories in this book are based on fact. However, the identities, circumstances, and locations have been totally altered to make any individual or place completely unidentifiable. In this way, both the innocent and the guilty remain anonymous, leaving me free to draw on my experiences to inform, help, and inspire others.

The police stories, though, are absolute fact. The only change has been renaming the officers who were my partners on those adventures.

B-GIN
10-4
Sat

Personal Discovery

'You've got to have a little faith'

When my husband and I parted ways, I was emotionally shot to pieces. I'd ended a seven year marriage with only an inkling of how much of a double life my husband had led. Long after we split, I was to discover just how bad the situation had really been. All that time together suddenly meant nothing, as layer upon layer of lies and deception were peeled back. The only tangible entity left to me was my two children.

They say that every crisis is an opportunity in disguise, or every cloud has a silver lining. Well, looking back I can see that, but at the time I was more interested in uncovering the truth about my husband's betrayals than finding any deep, inner personal truths about myself. And it was purely a basic need to get on his case and expose his game that drove me to keep a cool head, pull all my professional experiences together, and do my best detective work ever.

My close friends soon woke me up to the fact that I had something to offer other people in similar situations. I could run a business using my abilities and experiences while helping other people at the same time. And that is why I created Detection Group.

I had started my career in debt collecting and repossession when I was eighteen years old. In those early days, I was young and bullet-proof. I even considered having a shotgun shoved into my face a bit of a laugh. At the time, I was repossessing a phone from a guy. When I arrived at his front door, he was very friendly to me, asking me to wait by the door while he went and retrieved the phone. When he came back with the shotgun and pointed it into my face, I just left. I was actually laughing when I got into my car, thinking he must have really liked that phone. Looking back, I'm shocked at how little fear I felt.

Two incidents occurred while I was in the debt collecting industry that affected me profoundly.

The first was early in my career when I was collecting outstanding invoices for the Queensland Ambulance Service. In those days, when someone used an ambulance, they were charged about $250 as a standard call out fee. If the invoice wasn't paid, it was given to me to call the debtor and chase payment. Some people would pay up quickly. Others I would have to keep onto month after month, until they had paid the outstanding amount. A few would just never pay. Some debtors I spoke to weren't happy with having to pay, particularly if someone else had called the ambulance for them in the first place.

In one case, I had a young female debtor, a drug addict who had overdosed. Someone had called an ambulance to take her to hospital. So every time I called her, we would have an argument about the bill. She told me she wasn't paying because she hadn't called the ambulance herself, and that was it. One day, when I told her that we'd have to serve a summons on her and obtain judgement, she got really upset.

'If you don't stop ringing me, I'll kill myself,' she told me, and hung up.

I had many debtors who said some really outlandish and aggressive things in an attempt to avoid paying. I diarised another call to her for the following month, giving her some time to calm down and think about it. When I rang her again, four weeks later, I tried to rationalise with her about making at least a small payment.

'Look, we need some money. Just a dollar. Five dollars. Something. Two hundred and fifty dollars is not a lot in the grand scheme of things. Do you want to risk stuffing up your credit history over that? What if you want to buy a house or a car some day?'

Again, she hung up the phone on me.

I thought I'd give her another month to think things over. People often come around when they consider how it will mess them up later down the track if they have an outstanding debt. Credit card and loan applications are that much harder to get.

When I phoned the following month, her mother answered. I asked for her daughter. The mother told me that her daughter had killed herself. At the time, I don't think I believed her entirely, or didn't want to. I requested that the mother send me the death certificate, so that the debt could be written off. When the certificate arrived, I remember telling myself that she hadn't committed suicide just because of the debt or my phone calls to her. She would have done it anyway, I knew that. But I kept feeling guilty whenever I thought about her. I thought about how lonely and desperate she must have felt. So for a time after that incident I worked at being hard and impenetrable. I didn't want anyone else to affect me that way again. Yet, to this day, I have never forgotten about her.

My second groundbreaking moment happened a few years later, towards the end of my debt collecting days, when I had to call a woman who had a substantial outstanding debt on a motor vehicle loan. As we talked, she told me her story. Her husband had left her and their young daughter about eight months earlier. While they were together, he'd put the finance for their car in his wife's name but, just before he left her, he wrote it off in accident. It wasn't insured, so he'd left her with the loan repayments, which she couldn't afford, and no car.

This woman had so much pride that she wanted to do everything she could to try and pay off the loan. She had other outstanding debts to pay too, and she was renting, and raising a daughter on her own. During our short phone conversation, I felt such a connection with her. I had never met her, and I never did, but through that one phone call, she unknowingly taught me a lesson about empathy, compassion and humanity, qualities I hadn't associated with being a debt collector.

At the conclusion of our phone call, she had told me that she was going to sell her engagement and wedding ring, and use the money to put towards the outstanding debt. I had accepted this repayment offer and ended the call.

I then sat at my desk for a couple of minutes and thought about her. I went for a long walk during my lunch break and thought about her some more. Back at my desk an hour later, I picked up the phone, and called her back.

'I want you to sell your engagement and wedding ring as discussed, but I don't want you to send the money to us. I want you to use that money to buy something really special for yourself and your daughter. You can now consider this debt to be officially written off.'

She started to cry, thanking me profusely and telling me that I had just changed her life. She didn't realise it, but she had already changed mine. From that day on, I lost the chip on my shoulder and decided that what I wanted to do most in this world was to help other people.

I went on to become a security officer, working at the Brisbane Domestic Airport, Brisbane Convention and Exhibition Centre, and Southbank.

Work at Southbank was exciting, precarious and graphic. I dealt with a whole range of issues including murders, rapes, drug overdoses, drunk and disorderly people, serious assaults, and paedophilia. Experiencing these situations firsthand certainly helped me when I later applied for the Queensland Police Service.

One of the most dangerous nights was one New Year's Eve when, just before midnight, a male police officer and I were trapped against a brick wall by a hostile crowd. We had been patrolling around the park, just keeping an eye on the people, when we suddenly turned around to discover we had been cornered by a gang of over forty girls. As they closed in, swearing and spitting at us, I thought that I, being the female, stood a good chance of calming things down. I stepped forward, holding my hands up in a non-threatening way, and asked the girls to let us through. It didn't work. These girls were hyped up and out for blood, yelling and spitting and then shoving us around more and more violently.

It's a very scary feeling being stuck in the middle of an aggressive crowd. They feed off each other. Courage and confidence can make them reckless, and situations can become ugly very quickly. In a crowd, it's also impossible to see if anyone has a syringe or a knife. With our backs pressed hard against the wall, I knew I had to do something before the girls overpowered us and managed to seize the officer's baton or gun.

'Just follow me and stay close!' I yelled to the police officer.

I stepped forwards and made a grab for the first girl's breast, feeling quickly for her nipple, and then twisting hard. Shocked, she screamed out and backed away. I took another step and smartly twisted the nipple of the next girl. The police officer followed closely behind me as I made my way, grabbing and twisting through the crowd, to safety on the other side. I can look back now and see the humour in the situation, but being stuck in that crowd was nothing short of terrifying.

Later, in the early hours of the morning when the park was due to close, I was with a contingent of security officers forming a human barrier to move people out. Our progress was made more difficult when two rival gangs started fighting, and we had to try and calm them down too. They were pushing and shoving each other all around us, and then things happened really quickly.

I suddenly turned to my right to see a male security officer, only two down from me, badly stabbed by one of the gang members. There was blood everywhere as people rushed to help and an ambulance was called. Our adrenalin levels soared, along with fear and anger, giving us huge strength to push the last of the gangs clean out of the park.

When we finished, at 6am, and sat down to have a beer, it really hit us. One of our own had been stabbed, and it could easily have been any one of us. He could have died, and the fact that he was one of the most gentle and caring security officers at Southbank made no difference when it came to mindless violence. It was a close call for him, and we were all delighted when he made a full recovery.

During my almost four years as a cop, following my security work, I was involved in some really appalling incidents. It wasn't until I sat down and started working on my business plan for Detection Group, that I really appreciated just how much experience I'd put under my belt over the years. I was certainly qualified to run my own private investigation agency, but I had one extra ace that I knew would really make it work – I was female. Over the course of my career I have found that women can really make a difference in certain situations. Generally we don't appear to be threatening, so it's easier for us to diffuse a flashpoint situation. We also tend to listen more carefully than men, as well as talk more effectively. Most of the upset people we deal with just want to have their two cents worth, and then they can calm down and understand what's being said to them. This approach – listening and then talking – was not only helpful when I was doing my process serving and repossessions, but whenever I've had to convince people, over the years, to do something they didn't want to.

When I started Detection Group, it was a long time before I could draw a line in the sand to protect myself emotionally. I would work with clients who were dealing with incredible grief, anger, and despair. There's little in life's experiences more painful than betrayal, and it cuts deeper when it's a loved one who's used the knife. In the beginning, having experienced all that personally, I was oversensitive. Sometimes I was too willing to involve myself in client's sadness, and this in turn brought back memories of my painful times. I've learnt to try to distance myself a bit, but not to a point where I lose compassion. On an almost daily basis, I'm privileged to hear clients' stories about their predicaments and torments. And I'm so grateful that they've come to me for help, because helping my clients always continues to help me.

I've often been known to comment that some private investigators are too callous or matter-of-fact about their work. I understand where they're coming from because I've been there too. Being dismissive about other people's suffering, hardnosed when it comes to extracting money or property, and a little too concerned about how much a particular job is worth, rather than considering the client's feelings, is considered par for the course for many investigators. But there is a middle path.

I dealt with more emotional grief in the first twelve months of running my business than in my four years of police service. Yet the Queensland Police have a number of counselling avenues for officers involved in traumatic incidents, or buckling under the weight of emotional stress. Sometimes officers need a good kick up the backside to get them to talk about what's troubling them, whereas others happily talk it out.

Unfortunately, there are still many frontline cops with deep emotional issues simmering below the surface, but at least there is a system in place that recognises that being exposed to traumatic and emotional situations creates stress of one type or another. And, ultimately, that stress will manifest in some other detrimental form.

In the private investigation sector, no such counselling support exists. There are no psych tests on offer to see how agents are coping, or trained professional counsellors lining up to dig through the morass of mixed up emotions and make it all right again. There's alcohol, and yes, I went down that rocky road for a while too. Unfortunately, the stereotyped investigator swigging from his hip flask in the old black and white movies isn't that far from the truth for some agents today. And there are still those who believe that letting it all hang out down at the bar after work is the best form of therapy.

So, who do you talk to? Where can you get help? I have my friends, but unless they're in the investigation industry, how can they possibly understand how I feel after a really bad day, trying to help a client with a distressing issue? Isn't it easier to crack open another bottle and talk about something more pleasant? It's hard to try to forget about the woman who found out this morning that her husband of thirty years has been living a double life with her best friend and is still sobbing her heart out at the end of the day. I still wonder, for days later, about how she is feeling.

It's sometimes difficult to deal with heart-wrenching cases, especially when I can relate to them directly from my own experiences. It took a long time before I realised that although I'm a strong person—and there's very little that people can do that will actually shock me anymore—I'm not made of steel. Far from it. I still need my friends and my loved ones around to keep everything on an even keel and in perspective.

Also, little by little as I recovered from my own relationship break up, I've learned to trust people again, and it's a better feeling than cracking open that second bottle of wine, that's for sure.

I have moved on from the inner conflicts of my personal life. I now work hard, focus on building my business, and make time to raise my two girls. I have met some absolutely amazing people along my path from the torment of separation to inner peace. Because these people have provided me with friendship, love, and unconditional support, I owe them infinite appreciation.

Not long after my separation, I fell apart in a really bad way. If it hadn't been for these people in my life, I wouldn't be who I am, or where I am, today. Being a single working parent is tough, very tough. And I take my hat off to every single parent out there doing it on their own. Life takes you on a journey, and sometimes you just have to have faith. How wonderful that Faith also happens to be my middle name.

A Regular Doctor's Appointment

'He's off to the doctor, but there's nothing wrong with him'

How many times do we accept what our partner tells us without giving it another thought? It might be something simple like popping down the road to the supermarket, or something more complex like going away on a business trip. We don't ask them if that's what they were actually doing, because that could mean an express ticket to the divorce court.

But at what point should we be suspicious that all may not be what it seems? Partners can be extremely secretive, even lie outrageously, when they're organising a surprise birthday party. Is this justifiable deceit? Of course it is. Well, what about the grey areas? Is lying to your partner about the state of your health justified by not wanting to worry them? Where does 'of course it is' become a 'maybe'?

Anne reckons she knows her husband, Bob, pretty well. Well she should, shouldn't she, after sharing twenty years of marriage? Living and working a cattle station about three hours west of Townsville has kept them in close proximity to each other 24/7. This type of job keeps a person nailed to the land, and there are not too many excuses for heading into town except for supplies and the odd knees up at the local hall. Most of their entertaining was done at home with friends.

So when Bob began to make regular bus trips to Townsville (he couldn't cope with city driving) to see his doctor, Anne became concerned. Bob is a big man with no small gut. But he keeps himself fit through continuous hard physical work, doesn't smoke, and when it comes to drink, enjoys just a couple of stubbies every evening after washing off the dust of the day. He had never complained about anything more than the odd back pain, but he'd had that ever since Anne had met him. And when she queried his doctor's visits, he said, 'When you get to my age you've got to have regular check ups,' which didn't quite fit with the easygoing attitude he'd always had about his health.

Every couple of months for about a year, Anne would watch Bob put on his carefully ironed jeans, checked shirt, and best akubra, and drive to the bus stop very early in the morning. She discussed all this with her best friend, Marge, who soon quelled Anne's fears that Bob might be having an affair.

'No woman would put up with that. Just seeing a man every month or two wouldn't work for long,' she told her. 'And there're no phone calls, text messaging, or talk of other people. Bob's still Bob, you've got to admit that.'

The nice thing was that Bob was always really attentive and considerate for a few days after being away for the day. He brought her presents from Townsville – a brooch, a scarf, and even a new plasma TV arrived for her the day after one visit.

Anne enjoyed Bob's thoughtfulness. The station had been a hard road for both of them, building it up from scratch, bringing up the kids and getting them to Uni, and weathering drought and flood. When the work day started before dawn they hadn't really much time for each other. She was falling exhausted into bed each night as Bob struggled over the accounts. When he came to bed, she hardly knew he was there.

The years had passed too quickly, and she was feeling a bit worn out. Maybe that's why she made a bit more of an effort to look nice when Bob came back from his Townsville trips. Or was it more because of the sense of unease she felt, despite Marge's assurances?

'Have him followed,' Marge joked one day, 'maybe he's leading a double life. You know, kids, house, and all that.'

Marge's humour played on Anne's mind. Finally she realised that she couldn't go on without knowing what was going on. That's when she contacted me.

Anne was guilt-stricken about calling me.

'I feel like I'm going behind his back, not trusting him. I'm the one being deceitful here.'

'Look,' I said, 'this situation is giving you so much worry, and you're probably not sleeping too well over it are you?'

'It's all I can think about now,' she told me.

'Well, at least you can put your mind to rest. He's not telling you everything, so you'll have to find out your own way. If he's not doing anything wrong, at least it'll put your mind to rest.'

On the next occasion Bob took another trip, Anne followed my instructions to the T. She took a couple of photos of him with her mobile, saying that she'd send one to the kids. She then sent the images to me, and I transferred them to my agent, Frank.

Frank is an exceptional undercover operative, and one of the ingredients of his success is that he's over sixty years old. Not only has this given him an amazing bag of life experiences, a great asset in this work, but he is also a chameleon, able to change his appearance with nothing more than a different expression and a pair of specs. As he says, 'Nobody takes a blind bit of notice of little old men. We can blend in because we can't possibly be a threat, and people outside our business expect to be followed by 007. They look right through us.'

When the bus pulled into the bus station, Frank was there to meet it. As Bob put his akubra on, Frank knew he had the right target, falling in behind him, and following from way back. When Bob jumped into a cab, Frank didn't panic. His son, Joe, was already pulling out from the kerb to pick him up.

Every agent has a particular skill, and Joe's is driving. A huge part of covert surveillance work is keeping tabs on people as they move from one location to another. Losing a person in traffic is easy and extremely frustrating, so Joe's extraordinary skills are a godsend.

Joe started his driving career in the police, driving patrol cars, and then went on to special duties. Now Joe is comfortable and happy behind the wheel of any vehicle, and sometimes the vehicles he has to use are very ordinary looking, just to blend in.

Bob's cab ride wasn't long at all. He was dropped off outside a brothel where he paid the cabbie and then went inside. Frank gave him ten minutes to get settled, and then followed him in. Again, Frank's age and experience worked for him. He's a real charmer when he wants to be.

'I'm looking for my mate,' he told the hostess. 'He's supposed to be coming into town today and I always meet him for lunch after he's been here, but my phone's buggered. He's a bit of a cowboy, did he book today?' He was told that Bob had booked by phone earlier that day and was already there. That was enough. Frank made himself scarce before he was offered a service.

Bob reappeared ninety minutes later, hopped straight into a waiting cab, and headed back to the bus station. Obviously there would be no gift for Anne this time round.

In fact, when Anne confronted Bob, his wanderings were severely curtailed for evermore. Bob was astonished that he'd been sprung, but that was nothing compared to Anne's anger. This was the last thing she'd suspected, although she later heard from friends that quite a few of the husbands had twigged to what was going on, but none of this had been repeated to her.

At first, Bob denied having been there, but on hearing that video footage was on its way, he admitted to visiting the brothel.

'But I couldn't get it up, so nothing ever happened,' he protested sullenly.

Anne called me.

'Is it possible to talk to the brothel and find out from the girl if this is true?' she asked.

Time and again this happens with clients. It's almost as if they want to find a way to excuse their partner's behaviour.

'No Anne, it's not possible,' I told her. 'But, tell me, is it acceptable to you that he went to a brothel, whether anything happened or not?'

'No,' she said, bursting into tears.

'And if he asked you if it's OK to go to a brothel as long as he doesn't get it up, how would you feel? Would you say yes?'

Anne began to focus on the issue. Bob's behaviour, for whatever reason and whatever happened in the brothel, was totally, one hundred percent, unacceptable. He'd been caught cheating, and although there may have been reasons that Anne could work through, there were absolutely no excuses.

Anne did work through the reasons, at first blaming herself entirely for Bob's needs to seek sexual relief elsewhere. She remembered that month after month she had rejected his advances. She was too tired, felt frumpy, or was already asleep. This was a long-term issue which had finally come to a head. And then she understood that she wasn't to blame at all. Sure, their poor sex life may have contributed, but when did she feel loved and appreciated? Only when Bob came back from a brothel, and was that good?

Anne did console herself with the fact that Bob had chosen a prostitute rather than having an affair. There'd been no emotional attachment to the liaisons, and there never is with prostitutes. Men don't give the emotional side of such encounters a second thought. They don't want to. That's why they go there. Sure, an expensive high class hooker can make a man feel extremely special over an entire night, but when it's over – poof – it's completely over.

Thanks to Anne's courage in facing the unknown, Bob and Anne came through OK. Later down the track, they even found some of it funny. They talked more instead of slumping in front of the TV every night, and had many more early nights. Anne lost weight and made an effort to look good, and Bob never, ever, went to Townsville again without her.

The Colour Purple

'Nobody will believe me'

Any physical abuse is inexcusable. We all know that, so why does it still go on? Or, more to the point, why do some people put up with pain and humiliation in a relationship when all they have to do is walk out the door? Are they stupid? It's hard to imagine that having your front teeth knocked out is an enjoyable experience, so why stick around in a toxic relationship? The awful truth is that it simply isn't that easy for some people to leave. Many abused people feel financially dependent on their partners, and fear the thought of stepping out on their own. Others are frightened that, should they bolt, the threats of further violence will become very real. And sometimes, in the twisted, convoluted depths of the human psyche, people become dependent on physical abuse and accept it for the associated 'rewards' it brings.

As a dental practitioner, Simon is one of the best, a top ranking specialist in the field of cosmetic dentistry, and a principal of one the leading clinics in Australia. He is efficient to the point of ruthlessness with his staff, but always manages to have a kindly word for his patients as he soothes their nerves prior to treatment. His staff see his approach as a bit too mechanical, always expecting the highest standards of performance from everyone as he darts from room to room and one surgical procedure to another. However, he's incredibly good-looking and very charming, so when he becomes a little rude under pressure it's always easy to accept his cheerful apology when things have calmed down.

The staff often gossip about Jenny, his wife. She's a completely different kettle of fish. Timid and mousy to the point of being obsequious, she almost creeps into the practice offices on the rare occasions when she visits. Looking around nervously, she never asks for her husband, just drops off whatever she has and quickly leaves. They wonder what sort of relationship they have. After all, they are so different.

There was a time when Jenny was very happy. Meeting the incredibly cool Dr Simon before he went into his own practice was the highlight of her life. It was at a party at another dental clinic across town. Back then she was a senior dental nurse, working in the same building as Simon. Young to have such a responsible job, she took her duties seriously, deftly organising staff rosters, ensuring supply stocks were maintained, and, from time to time, soothing the egos of her practitioners.

Jenny had a reputation as the ideal senior nurse, and that's why Simon had cornered her at the office building party.

He made her an offer to jump ship. She refused. Her loyalty was important to her, she replied, and that was something that impressed him.

They were married six months later. There hadn't been any doubt in Jenny's mind. Simon was strong, positive and forceful in his opinions, and extremely ambitious. She enjoyed his leadership, allowing herself to go with the flow. It was good to have someone else make the decisions for a change. Anyway, why argue just because she didn't exactly see eye-to-eye all the time? Making a few compromises here and there didn't hurt.

A year after they were married, they had their first child, followed by a second exactly a year later. Suddenly Jenny was a very busy mum and her priorities changed from a successful professional life and running around after Simon, to focussing on the children. And that's when the relationship between them began to develop cracks.

Conscious of attending to the children's constant needs, Jenny assumed that Simon would be sympathetic when the house wasn't exactly immaculate, or when she'd forgotten to get the right wine for a dinner party. But he wasn't at all interested in excuses. In his highly organised world everything had to work like clockwork at all times. That's why he'd married her, he told her one night, prodding her sharply in the stomach, to keep things ticking over in a well-oiled, efficient manner. Nothing else mattered, he insisted. Jenny agreed. She would try harder to get it right.

Over the following four years, the criticisms became more frequent, along with sharp physical reminders of her failings. One morning, he punched her hip when she was slow to open the gate. It was just a glancing blow, but enough to result in a deep purple bruise that was sore for two weeks. Another day, he twisted her arm up her back for breaking a glass. It had simply cracked in the dishwasher, she told him. 'Liar!' he'd shouted, driving his knee into her thigh for good measure. One night, she'd gone to bed early, exhausted from a tough and noisy day with the children, leaving Simon to watch TV. She awoke to find him savagely pummelling her head and shoulders with a pillow, his face contorted with rage.

'What have I done?' she gasped between wallops.

'Get up you lazy moron!' he yelled. 'There's no cheese. You know you're supposed to get cheese.'

He continued to swing the pillow at Jenny as she dressed and grabbed her purse. Rushing out the door to the car, she caught her foot, tearing off an unlaced sneaker. She felt Simon close behind her, his breath wafting across her neck. She ducked just in time. A pottery mug grazed her hair before shattering on the drive. Jenny was in the car and careering wildly down the road before she realised that one foot was bare and bleeding from stepping on the shards.

It was almost midnight and very cold when she got to the local all-nighter. Limping, shivering, and sobbing quietly to herself, she weaved through the aisles, desperately looking for something Simon would like. The attendant watched her carefully, muttering to himself as he saw the bright red smudges of blood appear on his recently mopped floor.

Relieved, Jenny found two wedges of cheese she knew Simon would like. As she handed over the money, her hands shook madly. Shock had begun to set in.

The house was quiet when she got home and she found Simon asleep in bed. As she put the cheese away in the fridge she saw that the dairy compartment was full. There were seven different cheeses there, all the regular ones that Simon insisted on having, plus a couple more.

Jenny didn't know what to do. Simon's attacks could stem from anything or nothing at all. Sudden savage onslaughts would leave her sprawled across the floor, the children cowering in fright. Simon was careful not to mark her face, although her arms and upper torso were so severely bruised that in warmer months she had to put up with long sleeves and jumpers to avoid embarrassing questions.

That's when Jenny called me. She realised that she had nobody to discuss this with. She had searched for my website after an interview I'd done for the ABC. At first she was hesitant and anxious to make sure Simon would never know of our conversation. 'Could she leave him?' I asked. Jenny didn't know. He was bullying and violent sometimes, but often loving, generous and kind too. She knew she still loved him, and that was the problem.

I arranged to meet Jenny personally. Sometimes I think it's a good idea to be one-on-one when sensitive issues are being discussed. I feel more supportive and the client can see that in my face. I've been through an abusive relationship. I knew where she was coming from, and felt her pain. I wanted her to know that.

In a quiet coffee shop, Jenny showed me some of her bruises. Her arms were a mass of muddy yellow patches where Simon had gripped her before shaking her almost senseless the previous week.

'Georgie, our eldest, was so upset,' Jenny said, brushing away the tears, 'she clung to Simon's leg this time, screaming for him to stop. I was terrified he was going to hit her, but he didn't. He has never touched the kids, but I'm afraid that one day …'

Jenny still wasn't sure whether she wanted to leave. Uppermost in her mind was her concern about credibility.

'If I leave him, what will people think? I've never talked to anyone about this, so why should they believe me? He's so wonderful with people. He's always charming and caring. They'll never believe he's been doing this to me, and for so long.'

My job wasn't to convince her of one course of action or another. Jenny would have to work that out for herself. My brief was to give her the freedom of choice. It was simple – with evidence she had power, power to face her tormentor and negotiate, or power to leave him with dignity, and with indisputable proof that her claims were true. With evidence of her mistreatment, she would have a level playing field and hope for the future.

I photographed Jenny's bruises, and not only on her arms. Her whole body was covered in patches of discolouration ranging from a sickly yellow to a vivid purple that was extremely painful to the touch. Next we brainstormed through a list of counsellors I'd put together to find the person she could confide all this to. It was difficult. Jenny's sense of failure made her feel totally inadequate, and she still believed, at some level, that she was the one who'd done wrong. I ran her through the digital pictures we'd just taken, zooming into some lesions on her back.

'Is this something you'd expect anyone to put up with?' I asked.

Tears welling in her eyes, Jenny made her choice, picked up her phone, and set up an appointment for that afternoon.

The next step was to gather indisputable evidence. We would need a couple of hours to set up video and audio surveillance in Jenny and Simon's home. And that's when we ran into a problem.

Simon announced that he was taking a two week holiday, to relax and do some overdue work around the yard. Simon could afford to employ a maintenance contractor, which he did for the lawns, but his bush walk at the back of the property was his special project. 'It helps me to unwind,' he told their friends.

This was contrary to Jenny's experiences. The last time Simon had taken a break to fix up the bush walk had been the worst week of physical abuse ever. At one point, he'd come raging up to the house, his face scarlet with indignation.

'Where're my secateurs?' he demanded, rapping her sharply in the breast.

Terrified, Jenny could only shake her head. She didn't do gardening. She hated it. There was no conceivable reason for her to have had the secateurs, or any bit of gardening gear for that matter.

Simon punched her repeatedly in the stomach until she lay gasping on the floor. Then, dragging her to her feet, he shoved her into the small storage cupboard under the stairs. It was dark, with just enough space to curl up in a foetal position. Breathing heavily, her mouth was quickly filled with dust and grit. She heard the bolt snap shut.

'Stay there until you remember where you've put them, then.'

It was four hours before Jenny was allowed out. Filthy and dehydrated, she'd showered and gone straight to bed.

This time around, Jenny was seriously dreading Simon's holiday, so we had to work fast. We were ready when Jenny called to tell us that Simon was going to a large hardware store with a huge list of supplies. The drive there and back alone would take two hours – we were made.

Simon had just left when we parked in the road. There were just two of us, looking very relaxed and informal. My tech, Maree, stuffed her pockets with the gear she'd need and handed me additional stuff to cram into my large handbag. We didn't need the neighbours pondering over a couple of visitors with wires hanging out of their ears.

We got to work straight away and were doing well until I heard a car door slam nearby. That was too close, I thought. Jenny appeared from the kitchen, her face a pasty white colour.

'It's Simon. His car's in the drive.'

I pointed to a place on the sofa next to me. 'Sit here! Now! Quickly!'

Maree knew what to do. We have to be prepared for these eventualities. As I heard Simon's key in the door, she leapt into a chair close to us. I already had my laptop out, facing Jenny and myself.

'I'm Pam, we're doing a street survey, nice and simple,' I whispered, pointing at the screen.

'Jenny, where's my wallet?' Simon's voice was brittle with a hint of curiosity. He obviously knew there were strangers in the house.

He appeared in the lounge room doorway, staring at us. I held my breath. This could be very difficult for all of us and potentially disastrous for Jenny.

I jumped to my feet and went over to him, my hand extended. He took it automatically.

'Hi, I'm Pam. We're just doing a survey and your wife's saving us from the heat out there.'

I saw Simon's face tighten, his eyes flicking from Jenny to me.

I leaned forward slightly. My low cut T shirt wasn't exactly skimpy but when I saw Simon's eyes travel downwards, I knew it was enough to distract him.

He smiled. 'Yeah, well, what's it all about?'

Jenny came in on cue. 'Hi darling, I'm sorry, your wallet's on the table there. Pam's just about to start. It's all to do with preschoolers. Do you want to join in?'

I cringed. Maybe that would be going too far. I did have a survey on the laptop, but it wasn't about preschoolers and, in any case, we needed Simon out of there. Little did I know that Simon's pet nightmare was surveys of any kind.

'Um, no thanks, I'll get going, nice to meet you,' he said, as if he really meant it. He certainly was charming. He retrieved his wallet and then paused by the door. 'Just make sure you don't buy anything, Jenny.' There was a faint menace in his tone. We all knew that he meant it.

When Simon left, we looked at each for a moment and said nothing until we heard his car reverse out of the drive.

'Oh, God,' Jenny said, in a rush of breath, 'I thought I'd had it.'

'No way,' I said, secretly relieved. 'Nice work everyone. Let's get into it.'

Ninety minutes later, we were finished. Except for the main bedroom, bathrooms and toilets which Jenny didn't want under observation, surveillance cover was throughout. Jenny would have her evidence when Simon laid into her again.

Fortunately, the attacks on Jenny over that two week period of Simon's holiday were low-key compared to many others she'd experienced. But they were clear evidence of assault, involving rough pushing and shoving, punching, and arm twisting. At the end of that time, she'd had enough. Her courage and resolve had grown. At first she seriously contemplated confronting Simon with everything she had – photos, her friend as a witness, and the video records. Perhaps he would stop mistreating her. Suddenly she realised that this wouldn't be good enough for her. She woke up one morning and looked at her battered body in the full-length mirror, packed, and left with the children. There was a package for Simon on the dining room table that would give him a lot to think about for many, many years.

And Jenny was free.

A Hands on Approach

'Who's got my dick?'

I was a first year constable doing a 6am to 2pm general duties shift with a male partner, Mike. It had been a routine shift, filling out break and enter reports, attending traffic accidents, and just conducting general patrols around the area.

Throughout the morning, we received a few reports of thefts from schools. On three occasions, purses had been stolen from teachers' handbags, which were located in the staff rooms. We had been given a description of a male Caucasian, on foot, so we were on the look out for him during our shift.

But by the time we arrived back at the station, just before 2pm, we hadn't spotting him during our patrols. Mike and I had both locked away our firearms, and Mike had removed his utility belt. I removed my radio and was just about to take my utility belt off when a call came through to the police station reporting that the suspect had been spotted less than two blocks away from our station.

We looked at each. We both knew the starting shift wouldn't be organised and ready to deal with the situation for quite a few minutes.

'Let's go,' I said, and we took off, jumping into the police car we'd been using, and headed down the road with Mike driving.

Sure enough, right around the corner, there was our suspect wandering along the footpath next to a park. We both instantly recognised the guy as he was a known offender with a history of violence towards police. We also knew that he had Hepatitis B[1], so we would have to approach him very carefully.

Mike stopped the police car just in front of him, and I hopped out of the vehicle.

'How're you going?' I asked, stepping towards him.

---

1   Hepatitis B is the most common liver infection in the world and is caused by the hepatitis B virus. The hepatitis B virus enters the body and travels to the liver via the bloodstream. In the liver, the virus attaches to healthy liver cells and multiplies. This replication of the virus then triggers a response from the body's immune system. People are often unaware they have been infected with the hepatitis B at this stage.

The liver is the main site of hepatitis B viral multiplication. Hepatitis B infection can lead to cirrhosis (scarring of the liver), liver cancer or liver failure if it is not diagnosed and managed.

Worldwide, there are an estimated 350 million people with chronic (lifelong) hepatitis B infection, with the majority living in the Asia-Pacific region. In Australia, it is estimated between 90,000 and 160,000 people are chronically infected with hepatitis B. Between 1991 and 2005, there have been over 90,000 people diagnosed with chronic hepatitis B in Australia. (source – Wikipedia)

Instead of replying, he swung his right fist at my face, connecting with my jaw. I only just managed to turn my head enough to deflect the force of the blow otherwise I would have fallen to the ground. I started to struggle with the offender, taking him to the pavement with me. He then scurried free, got up, and ran into the park.

Chasing after him, my adrenalin was pumping, so it didn't take long to catch up with him. I dived for him in a full, headlong tackle. Down we went. By that time, Mike had called in for assistance and was there to help me. The offender had got to his feet again. He was strong, really strong, and obviously on some sort of drug. His pupils were dilated and he was very powerful. Some illegal drugs can give a person incredible strength, which makes restraining them very difficult and dangerous.

Mike wrapped his arms around him from the back and held him in a tight bear hug, giving me the opportunity to slip one handcuff bracelet onto his left wrist. I then had to find a way of fastening the second bracelet to his other wrist, and with Mike holding him in a bear hug, this was extremely difficult.

I moved across in front of the two struggling men. Just then, the offender, with a violent jerk, broke his left arm free from Mike's grip, and he swung his left fist at my head. His left wrist still had the handcuff bracelet attached and the other handcuff bracelet dangling free. I didn't have a chance. The spare handcuff bracelet connected with my right temple and everything went black as I fell to the ground. I went unconscious.

I don't know how long I was out, but when I came to I saw the offender lying face down on top of Mike who was flat on his back on the ground. It took me a few moments to realise where I was. Struggling groggily to my feet, I staggered over to see that the offender was biting Mike's right upper arm. I could see that he had broken the skin, and blood was flowing. I suddenly remembered the Hepatitis B. I had to do something to stop him, and I needed to do it quickly. I didn't want to use my baton on him as he probably wouldn't feel the pain anyway due to his drug induced state, plus I was concerned that he may get it off me and use it against us. That could be fatal. I was very concerned for Mike's health, so I did the only thing I could think of that would get the offender to stop biting.

I jumped onto his back and reached around his waist with both hands. I felt around until I found his penis, slightly engorged, most probably by the drugs and adrenalin, and bent it in half as hard as I could.

Suddenly there was a snapping sound[2]. He stopped biting and screamed, 'Who's got my dick?! Who's got my dick?!'

At that point, a taxi driver who was an ex cop, and an off-duty police officer who happened to be driving past, ran over

---

2 Known as a penile fracture, this is a severe form of bending that occurs when a membrane called the tunica albuginea tears. There is usually a loud popping sound followed by severe pain.

to help us. By this time, the fight had gone completely out of the offender, and he was easily restrained and handcuffed.

We had our day in court, but the offender was acquitted of any offence of assault against me or Mike. This was my first court appearance as a police officer, and I was very disappointed with the result. But sometimes, no matter how hard you work to put a case together for a court hearing, the bad people can still walk free.

Fortunately, Mike was later cleared of any infection.

Under the Microscope

'I don't want to confront my friend again'

It would be reasonable to assume that once a partner is caught cheating, the relationship is all over. And, by the time I've been invited to the party, that's usually the case. Why? Because in most situations where I become involved, it's too late. Partners are caught up in webs of lies. A cheating partner is quite often given the opportunity to 'fess up, either by direct confrontation or gentle questioning, and yet some make a conscious decision not to admit to anything. They're evasive, angry and blustering, lie outright, or try to deflect the accusations right back with counter allegations. That denial becomes a deeper form of betrayal. And then, when a partner continues to break the rules, the hurt is transformed into anger.

So, have all those years together been wasted? Not necessarily. An early and open admission of wrongdoing can often result in a salvaged relationship. If the erring partner comes clean and both partners are still committed to the relationship, there's still a good chance of it surviving. It's not an easy path. Not only has there to be a firm commitment on both sides, but trust has to earned. Imagine how difficult that can be. And the repair time isn't likely to be a five minute job. More realistically, it will be at least a couple of years.

Even in the early stages, there are telltale signs that a partner may be cheating. Each sign taken individually may indicate very little. However, collectively, suspicion begins to take form. For instance, it's reasonable that if a partner feels fat or frumpy they may decide to start going to the gym. But combine that with a different hairstyle, new and flattering clothes, working late, more business trips away, checking the mobile or email more frequently, and unusual credit card purchases or ATM withdrawals, and another perspective emerges. A cheating partner may not be silly enough to come home reeking of the scent of sex or a strange perfume, but not realise that the smell of fresh soap is a dead giveaway.

It's difficult for an affair to evolve without communication between the parties. Both SMS messaging and mobile emailing have made this easier. On the other hand, it's a great deal harder to conceal. There's usually one person in the affair unable to help themselves, needing to keep in touch, leaving an indisputable trail of (often quite explicit) evidence.

And is it the thrill of the chase, the excitement of a dangerous liaison, or an inherent psychological need that makes a cheater mention their lover's name at home, to talk about them somehow, and perhaps weave them into conversations in absentia?

From the beginning of an affair, there are clues that it's happening. Sometimes they're obvious, sometimes life is too busy for them to be noticed, and sometimes they're simply ignored.

Sally and Tim have been living together for eight years. Tim wants to get married and start a family, but Sally's not so sure. She hasn't entirely recovered from the huge bust up their relationship suffered three years back when Tim admitted to sleeping with her best friend, Dana. Sally finds it strange that she now trusts Dana again but is not entirely convinced that Tim wouldn't stray. She can't put her finger on the reason – it's just a weird feeling.

When Tim was caught out, he was quick to admit to the affair. Sally had absolutely no idea anything was going on until one night when he'd been particularly thoughtful in their lovemaking. As a silly joke she'd sleepily said, 'Who's been teaching you new tricks, lover boy?' She'd heard Tim's sudden, sharply drawn breath followed by absolute silence. Her cosy, post-coital warmth instantly turned to ice.

'Tim, what's going on?'

Tim was in tears almost immediately. Blubbering through his confession, he told her that Dana had run into him one Friday afternoon near her apartment, and invited him in for a glass of wine. Within an hour they'd opened a second bottle.

'After Dana showed me some of her ex's porn movies, one thing led to another. At first we were just kidding around, trying some of those ridiculous positions with our clothes on. Then, out of the blue, we started kissing …'

Sally had left Tim that night, returning to her parents' home. Dana and Tim had been keeping up their Friday afternoon sessions for over a month, even though Dana had found another boyfriend.

It took three months and a few in-depth discussions between the three of them before Tim and Sally got back together again. Both culprits assured her that they'd done a stupid, inconsiderate thing, and that there was nothing more in it than a dumb fling. And the hardest thing for Sally was to trust Tim again. She knew she had to if the relationship was to work. Gradually they both put the affair behind them, and, apart from Sally's odd niggling doubt, all was well. Until she felt a burning sensation when she urinated.

When she received her test results, she called me. Her voice was vibrating with barely suppressed anger.

'Chlamydia, he's given me effing Chlamydia. I want to know who it is this time.'

When Sally calmed down a little, she told me that she didn't want me to find out if Tim was having an affair or sex outside of their relationship. It was obvious that he was. She didn't want surveillance done on him. If he was seen going to Dana's apartment, that wasn't conclusive enough for her, because she was a friend. She had to know if it was actually Dana he was sleeping with. If it was anyone else, she didn't care. With her firm decision to ditch Tim anyway, the state of her friendship with Dana was all that concerned her now.

We were in luck. In the week following our phone conversation, Tim's movements were unaccounted for on only one day, the Friday, strangely enough. That night, while Tim was cleaning his teeth, Sally scooped up his undies from the laundry basket, dropping them into a paper bag. She would give those pants to me when Tim went for his swim later that day, and I would arrange to have the material tested for DNA profiles. We already had a cheek swab from Sally to eliminate her DNA from the results. That was the easy part. The next stage would be more difficult.

We needed a sample of Dana's DNA to compare with the profiles on Tim's undies, to look for evidence of intimate contact between them. DNA samples may be obtained from many sources. We just had to find the right one. Dana wasn't a smoker, so cigarette butts were ruled out. And Sally couldn't easily find an excuse to ferret around her friend's apartment looking for suitable items of clothing, hair, nail clippings, blood, or filch her toothbrush without arousing considerable suspicion. Most of these samples had to be fresh and related to Dana alone before the evidence was conclusive. If someone else had used her toothbrush, for example, the evidence would be skewed by contamination. Sally and I talked over the possibilities and then put our thinking caps on.

Within days, Sally called me. I could tell by the tone of her voice that she was onto something. Tim had just emailed her to say that Dana had invited herself and her new man, James, around for a game of Scrabble that coming Sunday. At first, Sally was concerned that she'd be spending the evening watching Dana and Tim for signs that they were at it again, but then she'd remembered something brilliant. The last time Dana was round at their place playing another board game, they'd made fun of the huge pile of tissues she'd amassed by constantly blowing her nose. Good-naturedly, Dana told them that she wasn't about to give them all a deadly virus, it was just the carpet setting off her allergies.

Could a DNA sample be obtained from nose mucous? It certainly could, and one thing was for sure, nobody would be likely to share those used tissues with Dana.

On the Sunday night, the collection went like clockwork. They had a great time, and James seemed like a really lovely guy. Sally kindly scooped Dana's tissues into a paper bag halfway through the evening, quietly sealing it and dropping it into the back of the pantry.

Sally's instructions to me were unusual. When the results came through indicating whether the DNA sample from Tim's undies and Dana's tissues matched, I was to give her a sealed written report of the findings, without giving her any verbal indication of whether the samples matched or not. In other words, Sally didn't want me to spill the beans before the report was opened. She wanted to walk away from me with the report in her hand, and without the slightest idea of the results.

One week later, after I had handed in the report, Sally, Tim, Dana and James met for lunch. About halfway through the meal, Sally took out both reports, opening the one I'd given her for the first time. The others watched her curiously. Sally's face hardly moved as she scanned the report.

'So Tim, who're you having it away with this time?'

Everyone was very, very still. Tim's voice seemed unusually loud.

'Sally, for chrissake, what are you talking about? We're supposed to be having a nice lunch here.'

Dana was staring fixedly at Sally's face. She was very pale. When Sally glanced at her briefly, she saw Dana almost imperceptibly shake her head.

Sally pushed my first report, the one detailing the samples found on Tim's undies, towards him. She was beginning to feel very angry.

'Pick up your mobile and car keys, and take this outside to read. Then, if you dare, come back in and sit down. Otherwise get your crap out of my place right now. And, by the way, Tim, as you seem to be so into freebies these days, lunch is on me.'

Tim began to speak, but Sally cut him off, pointing at the door. Food completely forgotten, they watched him go. When it became clear that Tim wasn't coming back, they turned to face each other. Sally reached across the table to give Dana's hand an affectionate squeeze.

'You and James enjoy your lunch. I think Tim will take quite a bit of stuff, so I think I've got a little shopping to do.'

What Sally had done made her feel better. She was devastated that Tim could have been so cavalier about their relationship, but knew that as far as infidelity is concerned – it's definitely two strikes and you're out. Tim was out when he dropped his undies into the laundry basket, but where was Dana in the one or two strikes department? Sally's approach gave her the final silent proof of Dana's friendship.

That night Dana appeared at her door with a bottle of champagne in each hand.

'Thought you might like some help unpacking your new goodies,' she giggled.

Sally passed her a large box of tissues.

'You're going to need these with all this packaging! C'mon, let's get into it.'

Author's note: Although we're all unique, because we're human beings with similar characteristics like arms in place of wings, most of our DNA is the same as anyone else's. It is only tiny polymorphic[3] portions that are actually unique to each individual. DNA profiling is basically separating the unique portions from the common ones and then comparing the unique samples. And can we still be 100% sure of the results? Because of chance, the answer is no. Results can only be 99.99% accurate, but for most people that's a pretty acceptable result.

---

3   Varying in shape.

Revenge

'I just wanted to get closure, to get even in some way'

On the surface, some of the things we're asked to do may appear to be very strange. A client's request to deliver a cricket bat along with some well chosen words would definitely raise a few eyebrows. But once you know the inside story it begins to make some sense. This was all about a woman who'd suffered at the hands of a physically violent man, and, years later, the trauma of the experience still haunted her. Her plan was carefully worked out as she'd thought about it for a long time, but she needed someone like me to execute it.

In her early forties, Lisa is small and willowy, quick on her feet, and reminds me of a dancer. I wasn't surprised when she told me that she'd had ballet training as a youngster and hadn't been permitted to continue because she'd never gained enough height. So she decided to go into the hospitality industry where she could dance her way around restaurants and get paid for it. Her precise, almost military work ethic constantly invited promotion to management but she was happy on the ground floor looking after her customers. With her dark hair and plain face, Lisa felt special, almost beautiful, in her work. She reckoned that her restaurant persona allowed her to blossom and be a little more out there with people.

Five years back, Lisa was married to Bill, an unemployed no-hoper. He wasn't interested in finding work, spending most of his time at the pub drinking his dole money and her wages.

It hadn't always been like that. He had seemed fine when they met. A bit rough, but appealing in an attractive, burly sort of way. His work in construction stopped soon after they were married. He'd been sacked from a number of sites for losing his temper and getting physical with the bosses, so it wasn't long before he had nowhere else to go. And that's when the violence started at home.

It didn't matter what Lisa said, Bill could always twist her words around to create tension that would end up in a huge argument. And, looking back, Lisa thinks she was looking for the excitement of a row too. It's almost as if she missed the attention Bill gave her in their early days and craved it to the point that she'd do anything to get a reaction from him. The problem was that it soon escalated from verbal abuse to pushing and shoving, and then to outright punching.

Soon Bill didn't need an argument to get physical. He'd come back from the pub angry, invent a reason, anything, like she'd left a cup in the sink, and then lay into her. She never fought back. He was too big and could have snapped her in half.

Then Lisa discovered she was pregnant. In the early days of their relationship, having children together was something they'd both talked about. They had wanted to start a family. So when she discovered she was pregnant, she was over the moon. It seemed heaven sent. Lisa thought it would bring them closer together, the abuse would stop, Bill would settle down, and everything would be fine. The afternoon she did the test and confirmed her pregnancy she was itching for Bill to get home so she could break the good news.

But Bill was later and drunker than usual. He stumbled through the door and lashed out. When Lisa screamed in fear for the baby, Bill became incensed with rage, went to a cupboard and hauled out an old cricket bat, a souvenir from his school days. He then pummelled her with the bat, swinging a really vicious blow to her abdomen. She was left lying in a dead faint while Bill took himself off to bed.

That night, Lisa lost the baby. She didn't say a word about the pregnancy or the loss to Bill. She just packed up and left for Melbourne the next day. And, for five years, she stayed completely out of contact with him, leaving no forwarding addresses. And that's when she contacted me.

Lisa had gone through hell since that last night with Bill, but with the help of counselling she felt she'd worked things out over the last few years. She was ready to move on, and needed to take one final step for closure. She wanted Bill to know what had happened during that final assault. That he'd caused the loss of their child and destroyed a life. When she began to explain what she wanted me to do, I expected her to ask me to pay him a visit with a bunch of heavies, which is obviously something we don't do. No, she was definite about the procedure, times, methods, the lot. No violence at all.

In fact, Lisa was totally cool and detached about what she wanted. Almost matter-of-fact, and her voice seemed remote and emotionless.

As Lisa had lost touch with Bill's whereabouts, I was instructed to track him down using our databases and other sources, keep surveillance on him to find out what he was up to, and then personally deliver a cricket bat to him with a letter and prepared speech. Lisa had taken a lot of time choosing the right sort of bat for him. The shopping expedition had been part of the therapy in a way. And when she discussed it with me we decided that it would be appropriate to gift wrap it too.

Bill was still in Brisbane, living with another woman and her teenage son, and he still didn't appear to be working. When I knocked at his door, a plain looking woman dressed in stained trackies answered.

'Is Bill about?' I asked.

The woman didn't seem particularly interested in me, just looked me up and down once before calling out for Bill. I was purposely dressed casually in jeans and a smart T shirt, and I was video recording the incident with a hidden camera, with another agent doing the same from his vehicle. The videos were needed because Lisa had wanted to see how Bill reacted as the news unfolded.

Bill came to the door, looking a lot fatter than Lisa had described him. He was unshaven and dishevelled.

'I've been hired to deliver this parcel and this letter to you,' I said.

'Who are you?'

I could smell the stale alcohol and cigarettes on his breath from a metre away. His eyes were yellowed and bloodshot with sleep still crusting in the corners. He looked very unhealthy.

'I'm just someone who's been hired to give you this stuff along with a message. And the message is that she was pregnant when you hit her.'

'Who?'

'It's all in the letter.'

'You obviously know who this person is?'

'Yes, I do. I've spoken to her. It's all in the letter, but I had to personally tell you that she was pregnant when you hit her.'

The strange thing about this encounter was that Bill was smiling in a confused sort of way throughout the conversation. As I walked away, leaving him holding the package, it struck me that perhaps he couldn't remember Lisa particularly, because he'd hit so many women over the years. But he certainly would have remembered when he unwrapped the parcel and saw the cricket bat. And he'd have to answer a few questions from his partner, as she had seen and heard the whole thing.

I called Lisa immediately to let her know what had happened, and to tell her that the video footage was on its way. She wanted to know how Bill had reacted, and what I thought he may have felt. I guess she had expected him to know immediately what it was about, instead of standing there with a half-baked smile on his face. But she was happy. She knew, as we spoke, that Bill would be working it all out and the letter would make it all absolutely clear. I could hear the relief in her voice. The tightness had lifted, and although she was in tears, they were tears of release. She could move on, and it was a job well done as far as I was concerned.

As Lisa moved on, I did too, at another level. I was beginning to connect the dots in my life, seeing how my early experiences had shaped my life, my decisions, and the people I became involved with – often to my detriment.

Fatal Car Accident

'He was in the way'

It was during my first couple of months as a new trainee that I attended a fatal car accident on the Freeway. When we arrived at the scene, the ambulance and fire department were already there, and the firies had managed to extinguish a serious car fire.

I had a talk with a witness who was very distressed. He'd seen the car hit from behind by another vehicle, causing it to roll a few times before landing back on its wheels and bursting into flames. The driver had tried to escape through the front doors, but had obviously found them jammed from the impact. The witness had then seen the driver trying to clamber desperately into the back to get to the rear ones, but had watched him die in the attempt.

When I looked closely at the burnt out vehicle, I saw the dead driver's body half way between the front and back seats. The body was so badly charred that all the clothes had been burnt away and I could see bits of brain and bones. As I tried to take everything in, my senses were overpowered by the smell. It was absolutely terrible, and to me very much like BBQ chicken, something I can no longer stomach, even now, years later.

After I'd organised an undertaker to take the body to the morgue, I went to talk to the other two guys involved in the accident, and who were suspected of causing it. As I walked over, I could see they were laughing loudly and joshing around. I was stunned. How could anyone be finding this funny, never mind the fact that they were probably responsible for the terrible death of an innocent person? I gritted my teeth.

'What happened here tonight?' I asked, calmly.

'Me and my mate were dragging, that's all. And that guy was in the way. Wasn't our fault he didn't get out of the way.'

Those words still haunt me today. Clearly those two were from another planet, with an entirely different set of standards to the rest of us. Sadly, there are people like that about, and I would meet many more before I finished my police service.

An hour or so after the accident, we discovered that the burnt vehicle was registered to a female, and although the firies were adamant that the body they removed from the wreck was male, we needed to confirm this before making enquiries so that we could inform the next-of-kin. Naturally the job fell squarely onto the shoulders of the new trainee – me.

It was 3am, I was in a morgue, and I was alone. To say the least, I was not just a little unnerved by the experience, I was terrified. I had to find the right gurney in the refrigerated area and look closely at a dead body. Now, given that a morgue is full of dead people, it should be a quiet place. But believe me, it isn't. Bodies release gases, making a sound like heavy breathing. It's very scary at the best of times, but for a young, raw recruit, it was awful. Over and over I told myself that these people were dead and not actually breathing again. It didn't help much.

When I found my crash victim, I checked and immediately saw a burnt penis. That was enough for me – I was quickly out of that place.

My next job was to pick up food for the officers still on duty at the crash site. As I stood at the food counter ordering the burgers, chips, and hot apple pies, the smell of the food on top of the stench of a dead body began to overwhelm me. I felt my gorge rising and wanted to rush outside to vomit. It was so bad I thought I'd never eat again.

Even after I'd delivered the food, finished my shift, and gone home, the smell stayed with me. I could wash my uniform, but I couldn't clean my police issue boots enough to get rid of that smell. It lasted for months. Every time I dressed for work, the stink was there to remind me of that night. Now it's just a memory, but an incredibly strong one that never, ever goes away.

The Bare Facts

'I thought she might be doing it for me, as a bit of a surprise'

People seem to put up with a lot in relationships. I've known men and women stick around when they've been beaten black and blue, married to alcoholics, serial gamblers, psychopaths, sex addicts, or just absolute no-hopers. And yet most partners draw the line at deception. Time and again clients come to me because they feel cheated, misinformed, and lied to. And that usually spells the end of a relationship.

Sometimes it's the most minor deception that starts the rot. Maybe not being truthful about meeting someone, a little lie about how much has been spent or about taking up smoking again. Relationships are about trust, or should be. A partner is someone we trust completely, until they let us down.

Steve works for the government, a good steady job with plenty of prospects and excellent working conditions. He's been there for three years and feels that his job is pretty secure and that he has opportunities for promotion. He's well respected by his colleagues, the bosses like him, and he's chirpy and cheerful – a great asset to the team.

Although Steve's been going out with Rachel for a couple of years, they still live separately, flatting with friends. At first they both thought this was a great arrangement. They had a bit of space apart some of the week to do their own stuff, and had each other to enjoy the rest of the time, going to parties, movies, or taking long weekend drives.

However, over the last few months there's been a shift in their relationship, and they've been spending more and more time together. It didn't take long before they both realised that living under the same roof would be the right way to go. Financially it made sense.

And then the discussions turned to the serious possibility of buying an apartment together. This was a huge turnaround in the way Steve and Rachel had thought their relationship was going. Suddenly they'd leaped from talking of sharing a home to actually owning one. They lost no time in checking out the possibilities.

This was incredibly exciting, but their euphoria was short lived. There was no problem with their combined incomes covering mortgage repayments. Steve's salary was pretty secure and on the move upwards. He'd almost have to commit murder to lose his job. And with Rachel being a teacher, her income was almost set in stone too. Between them, they had sufficient disposable income to afford a three-bedroom, near inner-city pad, perfectly located for work and entertainment.

The difference between the dream coming true and reality was $10,000, a seemingly impossible shortfall. And what was so frustrating was that the housing market seemed ready to go ballistic again, with house prices tipped to be on the move in less than a year. A miserable ten grand stood in the way of being able to put down a deposit, and how much had they frittered away in the last two years? Steve was an electronics nut, and Rachel loved new clothes. And what about that crazy holiday they'd had in Italy last year? What with car rentals, romantic Tuscan villas, and perfect candlelit dinners, it had taken the last twelve months to pay off the credit cards. For the time being, all of their plans would have to wait.

About two months later, at the end of a week, Steve was in the city bar he and his colleagues used for Friday night drinks. Some of the younger guys would make a real meal of it, heading off to a club until the early hours, but Steve, wanting a clear head for the weekend, would just enjoy a couple of schooners, and then head home.

They gathered at one of the trestle tables and started the usual good natured banter. This was the part of the evening Steve most enjoyed, and this particular night was no exception. Still wired from work, and looking forward to the weekend, everyone was in top form. Steve knew it wouldn't last. After four or five drinks the alcohol would kick in, reducing the quick wit into the bullshit and burble Steve found to be a waste of time.

He downed his second beer and checked his mobile for messages. Time to go.

'Hey Stevie,' one of the gang called. This was Cam, a self-confessed party animal, already onto his fourth beer. He'd be crawling home in the very early hours of Saturday morning. 'How did your birthday go, mate?'

Steve laughed. It had been his 27th birthday four weeks back. The guys had sent him home with a fair few more beers under his belt than he normally had. Luckily Rachel, with some school function on the go, hadn't been staying over, so his horrendous condition had passed unnoticed. Cam had been on leave since then, missing the tail end of the story and assuming Steve had been in real trouble when he got home.

'Nah, mate, Rachel wasn't there, so you wasted your dough. And I was up bright eyed and bushy tailed the next morning for our weekend up the Sunshine Coast.'

'And how did the pole dancing go, mate?' Cam asked, nudging one of the blokes sitting next to him.

'What pole dancing, idiot?' Steve replied.

The group broke into gales of laughter.

'Don't worry, Stevie, we know all about it,' said Cam, still laughing, 'Me and Dave were coming round by The Exotica one night just before your birthday, and ran into Rachel coming out. She gave us the drum, mate, taking pole dancing lessons as a surprise extra birthday present for your weekend away – what a woman. C'mon, you can tell your mates. How was it?'

Steve was silent for a moment, his head spinning in ninety directions at a time. Pole dancing? Surprise? The Exotica? Luckily the guys were too busy cackling and already too pissed to notice his confusion. But they were still expecting a reaction.

He forced a laugh. In his head it sounded hollow and sickly.

'Hey, what goes on in the privacy of the bedroom fellas …'

Steve picked up his phone and grabbed his bag as the guys jeered good-naturedly.

'See you Monday,' he called over his shoulder, hardly daring to look at them.

Outside, Steve allowed the cool air to wash over him. Something wasn't right. If Rachel had been taking pole dancing lessons for a surprise birthday gift, why hadn't she delivered it? Steve's mind flashed back to that weekend in Mooloolaba. As weekends went, it had been quiet. They'd spent heaps of time sleeping and mooching over coffee and the weekend papers. Rachel had been exhausted, so the extra rest suited him fine. But there certainly hadn't been a trace of pole dancing.

On the train ride home, Steve mulled it over. He could ask Rachel outright what the hell was going on. But he hated confrontations, especially with his feisty girlfriend. Only once before, when they'd just been seeing each other for a month or so, had he questioned where she'd been. And did she go off. Lecturing him about trust in a relationship, until he wished he'd never opened his mouth. He wasn't keen to have another dose of that, thank you very much.

Perhaps she hadn't got it right for his birthday, and was still working on it. He'd look such a dickhead. Why else would she have told Cam and Dave she was taking pole dancing lessons? If she'd been in the club for a giggle, she would have said so. Steve decided not to do anything about it for a couple of weeks, but, a few days later, something happened to change his mind.

Craig, one of the guys at work, was leaving to go overseas for two years. He had a brilliant apartment right in the hub of New Farm and, rather than give it up, was prepared to sub-let it to Steve and Rachel until he came back. The rent was decent, and it had a river view, something Rachel always wanted.

He couldn't believe it when Rachel was noncommittal about the deal. Steve had rushed around to her place to give her the news, and there she was, watching TV as if he'd asked what was for dinner.

'Are you kidding me, Rachel?' he'd asked. 'This is fantastic. It's in your favourite part of New Farm, it's reasonable, and it's got three bedrooms. What more do you want?'

Rachel looked up briefly and smiled tiredly, 'I just think we should wait a bit longer, that's all.' She yawned. 'Stevie, I'm buggered. It's been a long day, and I need to get some sleep. Let's talk about this tomorrow.'

Steve turned the TV off as Rachel closed the bedroom door. Was that it? He'd been so certain of Rachel's agreement that he'd given Craig a huge hug and told him they'd take it. This wasn't the Rachel he knew. Maybe she was seeing someone else and had new plans. Was it anything to do with that pole dancing stuff? It was all becoming far too complicated, and he had to know what was going on.

Steve called me, explaining his situation from the beginning. He was genuinely concerned about their relationship, but felt incapable of talking to Rachel about his misgivings. I told him we would find out what was happening and get back to him. Steve and Rachel still took time out of their relationship on Wednesdays and Thursdays, so that made things a lot easier for us. If anything was going to occur, it would be on those particular days.

When Steve emailed over Rachel's photo and work details, I assigned the job to Max. Quietly spoken, and totally unassuming, Max is short and slim. Not that anyone would want to tangle with him. He's a master of martial arts and very, very fit. But in a crowd he's almost invisible and works hard to make it that way. Skilled in close quarter surveillance, he could be following me and even I'd have to work hard to pick it.

Max has had an eleven year run of success. 'That's not counting Murphy's Law,' as he wryly puts it. Buy him a beer on a night off, and you'll hear the story of the jaywalker.

Max made sure Rachel made it to school then he was back in position when she came out. It was a textbook follow as she made her way home in her car, parked, went into the Night Owl to buy milk, and then went inside her apartment. Max settled down. He had a feeling he was in for a wait, and he was right.

Several hours later, Rachel reappeared carrying a sports bag. Was she off to the gym? Max had checked my notes before he'd started, and there was no mention of keeping fit. This time, Rachel turned her car towards an area of Brisbane well known for its club life. Off for a night out with the girls then?

Max watched Rachel park in a quiet side street and walk back up towards the neon and glitz. She took a sharp turn down an alley and went into an unmarked door. Max wandered down the alley, got to the door, paused briefly, and then kept walking. The door was locked, so Rachel must have used a key.

Max knew the building was a 'gentleman's club', so after waiting fifteen minutes he went inside. This club was fairly classy with upmarket décor. Max paid his 'membership fee' to the bored attendant and went to the bar to order an incredibly expensive beer. There were two strippers coming to the end of their acts, gyrating to the rhythm of techno music. Max shuddered; jazz was more his thing.

There was a reasonably large clientele for a Thursday night. Max thought about a second beer, but dismissed it. He knew what I thought about excessive expense claims. But he didn't have to wait around long. Rachel appeared on the pole dancing catwalk, looking totally different to the woman he'd seen slip through the side door. In fact, it would have been very difficult for anyone to recognise her, even a good friend. She'd just been unlucky to be sprung on her way out by Cam and Dave.

Max watched for long enough to get the video footage I needed, and then left. He called me as soon as he was outside. She was good, very, very good. And Max reckoned she'd be getting paid top dollar, even as a newbie. No doubt that wasn't something Steve would want to hear.

Clients ask me if they should just go ahead and follow their partners themselves to find out what they're up to. I recommend strongly against it, for a number of reasons. Surveillance isn't something that can be picked up from reading books or watching movies. It's a highly skilled trade, where a mistake can be dangerous. Also following a partner and finding them engaged in, say, an extramarital affair, can create a highly emotive situation, and usually an unsatisfactory outcome for all. There are also legal and licensing requirements that need to be fulfilled to follow. In Steve's situation, it would also have been difficult for him to enter the club. Clubs actively discourage partners from being on the premises and will often automatically bar anyone personally associated with the strippers. The girls provide a list of names to management, and when those people show their ID at the door – bingo – they're refused entry.

When Steve confronted Rachel about the stripping, everything fell into place: the tiredness, her reluctance to discuss renting a place together, and why she was doing it. They'd needed only $10,000 to buy their dream home together. She had a friend who pole danced three nights a week and had scraped together enough money for a deposit in no time, so she knew she could do the same. She didn't dare suggest the idea to Steve because she reckoned he'd have gone off his tree.

In fact, Rachel was wrong. Steve, although initially surprised at the idea, would have been quite open to it as a short term project. He reckoned he would have pulled his weight too, by taking an evening job somewhere to speed things up. But as it turned out, Steve was devastated by Rachel's lack of trust, and what he firmly believed was deceit. He just couldn't get his head around the whole thing, deciding to call an end to the relationship. 'After all,' he joked months later, 'I believe relationships should be about honesty, and baring it all – well, you know what I mean!'

Secrets and Lies

'I just wanted to level the playing field'

Tracy wanted out of her marriage. After ten years, she felt she had let her life slide by. She didn't feel that her husband, Sam, was interested in her anymore, if he ever had been at all. She felt she was in a one-way relationship. She would come home from work with interesting titbits of gossip (she prefers to call it 'human interest') and end up feeling like she'd been talking to an empty box.

For years Sam had listened politely, and then, without much in the way of comment, gone off to watch TV, read a book, or do some work from the office. He was the senior accountant in a huge company, holding a powerful position, yet he never offered anything up to Tracy about his day. When she asked, he'd tell her he'd 'just been working, that's all'.

When they met fifteen years ago, Tracy and Sam were on a personal development course together. She was attracted to his charisma. He was funny and entertaining in a group, and although he didn't power dress like many of the other corporate types, he had a way about him that made people sit up and listen. At the same time, she was vivacious and witty, so they formed a natural social team. From there, they drifted into marriage and had two children, now aged ten and eight.

Tracy didn't consider herself particularly attractive, but she did keep fit, looked after her skin, and took care of her long, naturally blonde hair. Guys in the office really liked her, and in a considerate way. They didn't hit on her the way they did with the younger girls. These working relationships were more intellectual, she thought, more a meeting of minds. She felt she still had plenty to offer people in the way of friendship, and she was beginning to feel that she was missing out.

Domestic life was quite different to the corporate scene. Sam was quiet and introspective most of the time. He'd kept his rugged good looks, and now, with glasses, looked very stylish. But for all that, there was nothing there, for Tracy at least. Sam didn't even bother with conversation at the dinner table anymore.

In charge of the home accounts, he'd often be fiddling with his laptop. She had no financial worries; their incomes were extremely healthy. Tracy had no idea what Sam earned, but hers was top money, they owned their own home, and her credit card bills were taken care of, on time, without question. Not that she was spendy. Tracy had inherited a small fortune which they'd invested into some apartment projects, the details of which never interested her. She was careful with money, but didn't stint on essentials.

When Tracy emailed me, she simply said that she was intending to leave Sam, and wanted to know precisely what they jointly owned. When I asked Tracy what she thought their net worth would be, she was extremely vague. She hadn't kept track of their investments at all. Perhaps they owned two or three properties other than their own home, she wasn't sure.

Obviously feeling a little silly about her lack of knowledge, Tracy explained further. Over the last year, with a separation in mind, she'd been more interested in their assets, asking Sam about them from time to time. He'd surprised her with his evasiveness. She realised that he'd been looking after the accounts for years, but she didn't expect to be fobbed off when she asked reasonable questions. This made her think, and she realised how little she knew. In fact, she knew virtually nothing. When they separated, this would not be a satisfactory situation at all. Sam would have complete control over assets she might not even know existed.

Tentatively, Tracy had tried to pry into her own affairs, shocked at how little progress could be made. Drawers were locked, and from what she remembered, they always had been. She had always assumed they were locked as a safeguard against little children's fingers. So where were the keys? They certainly weren't where all the household keys were kept, on a hook, high up in the pantry. Not on his car key ring. So where? And why were they so well hidden?

Sam's laptop was her next mission. Whenever it was home it was never far away from him, but, fortunately, Sam slept like a log. Feigning a migraine one night, Tracy slept in the guest room, slipping out of bed in the early hours to switch on the machine. She didn't get far. The laptop required a password and, try as she might, she couldn't crack it with the passwords they usually used on their main family PC.

In the quiet hours of night, Tracy's mild concern turned to worry. She realised that she hadn't a clue about their financial matters, had never owned a cheque book, and didn't mess about with internet banking like the other girls in the office. Sam kept her ATM card well topped up, and she had her bottomless credit card, and that seemed to be enough – until now. She never even saw any statements, as Sam dealt with all that.

I asked Tracy to get some information for us to initiate our searches. We have access to databases, and there are many investigative avenues we can take once we have the basic facts. Usually things start to unravel quite rapidly, as they did in this case. Most partners who are hiding assets use their own names, names of lovers, or very good friends, to squirrel cash and property away. Using false identities can be very dodgy, as this begins to transcend lines of legality and creeps into areas of fraud. Obviously using a lover's or a friend's name can also be fraught with danger. On many occasions, the third party has taken off with the goodies, leaving the scheming partner in a very unhappy position. What can they do?

Gradually a picture emerged. Sam was running two bank accounts under his name alone which he used to transfer funds. He had managed to own three properties entirely in his name, and he had a substantial investment portfolio.

Clearly Sam was putting assets aside for a rainy day. But what precisely he had in mind, we'll never know. We found no evidence of another relationship, but that doesn't mean it wasn't happening. One thing's for sure – he wasn't intending to share those assets with Tracy.

When Tracy and Sam separated, it was interesting to see how much Sam declared as joint assets. It was quite a tidy amount. If Tracy hadn't known any better, she would have swallowed his assessment hook, line and sinker, thinking that they'd both done rather well. In fact, Sam had quietly retained twice that amount in his own name. Needless to say, the court was unimpressed with his financial acumen and took him to the cleaners.

It always pays to keep an eye on financial matters, even if you find this boring. It's not necessarily a matter of trust. We all trust our partners. If we don't, we shouldn't really be with them. But when relationships dissolve, trust, love, and respect dissolve with them. There are often only three matters left on the agenda – loathing, kids, and money. The division of assets should be legal, fair, and above board, and it so often is not.

Sex on Tap

'I want to know how far she'll take it'

The internet and mobile phone phenomena have revolutionised the way we interact with people. In ten years, our social networking and ability to communicate have expanded beyond our wildest dreams. It's hard to walk down the street without having to take responsibility for someone wandering along totally engrossed in a phone conversation, furiously texting, or listening to whatever.

Facebook, Twitter, LinkedIn, and MySpace are just four of the one hundred and forty seven better known social networking websites available worldwide at the time of writing. And there are many more. Many of them interact with each other, creating an even greater interlocking web of social activity. What do people use social networking sites for? The reason's obvious, isn't it? Or is it?

All this virtual interaction can change its form. Some interaction that starts in a virtual space later becomes physical. Cyber stalkers can solidify into physical stalkers, Knitters Anon may break their cover and meet up for afternoon tea, long lost friends and relatives become reunited, and offline relationships are born. It's all happening out there, and sometimes we can peek in for a look.

Matthew knows a lot about the internet. He's in IT, has his own business, and is working every hour under the sun to get established. He shies away from the sloppy geek dress code popular with IT people, favouring well-cut business suits. As his business expands, he's meeting new people all the time, and wants to look his best.

A little self-absorbed, Matthew doesn't have much time for socialising. The closest he comes is when he calls into a smart café for a caffeine hit and a quick scan of the business pages on his way to work. And that's how he met Sarah, one of the wait staff. They hit it off right from the start. She was smart, lively and funny, starting his long days off with the right vibe, and she was attracted to his self-deprecating sense of humour.

After six months of going out for the occasional movie and late night dinner, they moved in together and became engaged. They planned to marry after a couple of years when Matthew's business had become more stable, and looked forward to having children.

Matthew's work was a tough call on their relationship. He was determined to focus almost every working minute on his business, so it took a fair amount of effort on Sarah's part to live what she considered a halfway decent life, heading to the odd party, enjoying dinner with friends, or just going away for the weekend. It was a huge exercise to drag Matthew away from his work long enough to enjoy just some of these things together. She was young, vibrant, and alive, and yet she seemed to be spending more and more time at home on her own.

The day Matthew called me he'd just finished a meeting with his business partner, Jamie, and their accountant. Jamie was an old friend. They'd flatted together through Uni, gone their separate ways for a few years, and then re-established the friendship when they ran into each other a couple of years ago. Going into business together just seemed the sensible thing to do, and it worked.

As the accountant left the office, Jamie pulled Matthew to one side.

'Can I have a quiet word?' Jamie had asked him.

'No worries mate,' Matthew said, still leafing through the reams of documents they'd been discussing. 'This accounts stuff gives me the shits. Do you understand it all?'

'Nah, that's what we've got accountants for, Matt. We've just got to look interested. Hey, man, I don't want to interfere in your private life, but I've found out something you should know about.'

Jamie took Matthew into a small meeting room and shut the door.

'Bit serious aren't we mate?' Matthew asked, cautiously.

Jamie didn't laugh, which deepened Matthew's concern.

'Out with it then.'

'It's about Sarah, mate. I've been trying to find a way of letting you know what she's been doing.'

Matthew slumped into a chair. He didn't know what to think. Was she having an affair? His heart was bumping, and it wasn't helped when he saw Jamie open up his laptop and swivel it towards him.

'What's this?' he asked, now totally confused.

Matthew could see Sarah's face smiling back at him from the screen. He recognised the photo immediately. He'd taken it just after they'd spent the afternoon in bed at a beach house they'd rented for a rare weekend away last year. She looked absolutely gorgeous with her long hair messed up, cheeks flushed, and beautiful eyes full of lust and wicked humour. But what was the pic doing on Jamie's laptop?

'It's a dating site. She's on an online dating site, and she's saying she's single…unattached,' Jamie mumbled. 'Sorry mate, but I thought you should know. I was just doing my usual cruise for a date and came across her. Maybe she's just doing it for a bit of fun. You know, with one of her friends over a couple of glasses of wine or something.'

Matthew knew all about Jamie's dates. Time and again they'd discussed the way the internet had changed everything about meeting people. The "great leveller" Jamie had called it. And he should know – it was his social medium. Jamie wouldn't go to a bar or club to meet women. Noisy, stifling, and crowded, those places were meat markets. No, Jamie liked to find the right profile on a website, meet the person for a coffee, and, if all seemed to be going well after a few emails and text messages, take it from there. His social life was bulging at the seams, and he was always with someone interesting.

In the past, Jamie had told him about how some of the websites were used to cater for those more open about their sexual activities.

'It's about sexual freedom with no strings attached,' Jamie had explained. 'Men and women post their preferences there, either with their true details, or anonymously, and with photos. The sites can be for meeting people in the traditional conventional style, or to partner up for an afternoon's fun.'

'So, even women are happy to meet up just for sex?' Matthew had asked, astonished at his own naiveté.

'In ever increasing numbers, mate. There're loads of frustrated housewives, even high-powered corporate types, who want a bit of excitement but don't want the mess of an affair. I had a session myself, but she came on too strong for me. I'm not into bondage.'

At the time all that seemed to be fascinating, yet far removed from Matthew's own lifestyle. And now here he was in the thick of it. So what was Sarah after, he wondered, as he stared dully at the screen? He felt sick. He couldn't even bring himself to read what she'd put in her profile. Jamie folded up the laptop.

'Sorry, mate. But we've known each other a long time, and I couldn't not tell you. What do you reckon you should do?'

That's when Matthew called me. He was sure about one thing. He wanted to know if Sarah was seriously looking for someone to become involved with, or whether it was just a silly prank, as Jamie had suggested. To Matthew, the answer to that question was all that counted now.

Matthew sent me a detailed email. In it was everything he knew about Sarah, her interests, food preferences, favourite holiday dreams, books, movies, and music. We then set up the ideal partner as a trap. Our fake persona, Cameron, was perfect. His photo smouldered with sexuality, he had heaps of time on his hands, and almost identical interests to Sarah. We then sent Sarah an internet kiss to show Cameron's interest in her.

She responded within an hour. But we were careful not to be too enthusiastic, allowing her to raise the temperature over a few days. The internet is known to be rife with predators, so people need to be soothed into a relationship. Too quick and Sarah would have questioned Cameron's motives, too slow and she may have lost interest. We still weren't sure of Sarah's reasons for putting herself out there. Was she looking for a fling, or for something more permanent? We had to play it both ways.

Within a couple of days, it was clear that Sarah was very keen to meet Cameron. Our 'man' responded positively, and the tryst was arranged for a weekday morning in a trendy inner-city café on Sarah's day off.

During this time, Matthew made out to be absorbed in a particularly difficult stage of a new project, staying at the office until late each night. He told us that this suited him fine, as he really couldn't face Sarah until he knew what she was up to. He wanted to know if she'd actually go through with it.

In this particular case, the scenario was clear for us. We just had to use the information Matthew gave us to kick off an operation and discover the facts. But not all circumstances are so well defined. Jamie was right when he told Matthew about the meetings arranged over the internet purely for both partners' sexual gratification. Some like to feel they're living on the edge, or in the moment, when they arrange a one-off sexual encounter in a vehicle, motel room, or even a vacant property for rental or sale somewhere, and people race around to have lunch time sessions. It's a growing interest, much to the ire of the escort services, who view free, quick, no strings attached sex as a direct threat to their livelihood. And the health risks these sexual adventurers take is also a growing problem. In a hurried and excited encounter, precautions can be blown to the wind.

I'm asked many times how we can discover whether a partner is using sex sites. And, depending on the circumstances, there are many answers. We have extensive databases that we can correlate against phone numbers on file. We can organise ghost programs for computers, and key loggers that record where a user goes and what they type. And people just aren't careful enough. For instance, one husband left a folder called passwords on his desktop. And when he used sex sites, he used his own photo.

On the big day, we picked Matthew up from work and drove to the café. The meeting was set for 10am, a busy time, but we'd already parked a surveillance vehicle where we could see most of the tables. We all climbed into the surveillance vehicle and waited. By 10.05am, I heard Matthew let out his breath. She was late. The poor bugger was in a state, and even I was starting to feel nervous for him.

At 10.07am, Sarah appeared, walking from the direction of the train station.

'Oh, shit,' Matthew muttered, 'what a bitch.'

Sarah stood outside the café, staring around the tables before choosing one a mere four metres from us.

'Crap,' I heard Matthew say. 'She's even got a new outfit for him.'

We waited until Sarah had ordered her coffee, indicating that she was prepared to wait it out. She was looking around, and, as the time went by, she began to look disappointed. She was halfway through her coffee when Matthew, as arranged, got out of our vehicle and went to her table. At first, Sarah obviously thought that Cameron had arrived, as she turned to the figure standing next to her with a brilliant smile. Her joy and relief was wiped off her face in the next instant as she recognised Matthew. He sat down at the table, and turned briefly to wave as we pulled away from the kerb. Our job was done.

Sarah admitted to Matthew that she'd been looking for someone new. And what had started as a tentative dabble on the dating site had become quite an occupation. She'd been on a number of dates, even having short affairs with two people she'd met. She felt that Matthew was too engrossed in his work for her, their relationship was dead, and she was moving on. She just hadn't wanted to go before she had someone else, that's all.

Undercover Prostitute

'I'll pay you five dollars for a head job'

I spent nearly a year in the Prostitution Unit conducting surveillance on, and raiding, illegal brothels. Undercover, as a street prostitute in the red light district of Fortitude Valley, I passed many a night standing on corners wearing a short, tight dress and knee high boots. I had a listening device strapped to my body and wore a snub-nosed .38 in a thigh holster.

My boss parked in a vehicle somewhere close by to keep an eye on me, with a couple more undercover guys in an unmarked police vehicle nearby. Standing on the corner of Brunswick Street and a side street, I waited until a car approached with a guy in it. Usually he would drive past slowly the first time, looking at me, and then once more before stopping alongside. The conversation would be pretty brief and go something like this:

'Hi there.'

'Hi.'

'I'll pay you fifty bucks for a blow job.'

'Sure. I'll meet you down the end of the street and hop in down there.'

Usually the guys would do a U-turn, heading towards the end of the street, and I would start walking down the road, at the same time describing the car, noting the rego and giving details of the guy. All this was picked up on my listening device and recorded by my boss, along with the conversation, as evidence. Down the road it wasn't me the punter met but one of the undercover guys working with me. The punter would be told what offences had been committed and issued with a Notice to Appear at Court. Meanwhile, as soon as I'd seen that he'd been intercepted, I was on my way back to my corner to do it again. It was a pretty smooth operation, and I could end up repeating it twenty times a night, especially on busy weekends.

One particular Sunday night really stands out for me. It happened to be the last day of Indy at the Gold Coast, and it was the busiest night I had ever had in the unit. The boys seem to come away from the races all pumped up with testosterone and busting for some action. And, from what I saw, sex was a high priority.

During the evening, a sedan pulled up across the road with all its windows wound down, so I could see there were two guys in the front and three in the back. The driver leaned out of his window.

'Hey there!' he called out.

'Hi,' I replied.

'Come over here.'

When I went across the road to stand near the driver's window, I felt a bit nervous. This was unusual for me. I'd been approached by hundreds of different men while undercover and never felt concern. I couldn't explain why, but this time things didn't feel right. I had to remind myself that my boss was watching my every move and could hear everything that was said.

'Hi guys, what are you up to?'

'Just looking for some fun.'

Just then, one of the guys in the back leaned over and offered me a five dollar note.

'How about a blowjob for each of us for five dollars?' he asked.

'Sure,' I said, taking the money.

The offer was ridiculously under priced, but by offering to pay for a sex act he'd committed an offence. It didn't matter how much money was involved. We had him.

The guy in the back seat opened his door and swung his legs out.

'So what's your name?'

'Bambi,' I replied.

'Cool. So come on then babe, get in.'

He then moved his legs to the side to make space for me to climb in between him and the other two guys in the back seat.

It wasn't going to happen. One thing we never, ever do, is get into a vehicle.

'No,' I said. 'I've got a unit down the end of the street. I'll meet you guys there instead.'

Suddenly the guy grabbed my arm and tried to pull me into the back seat.

'Let go,' I said, pulling away. 'Do you want to get busted by the cops? They're always driving past. I told you, I'll meet you down the road.'

In these situations, I had a code word that would alert my boss if I needed urgent assistance. But I wasn't ready to use it as I felt that the situation was still under control. The guy from the back started to rub his hand up and down my legs. That had me worried. The problem wasn't the touching, it was my thigh holster. I didn't want him to find it, so I backed off slightly. He must have thought I was about to take off, because he grabbed me by my arms and tried to haul me into the back of the vehicle. As we were struggling, I felt a few hands grabbing at my legs, breasts and bottom, and I knew it wouldn't take long before one of them felt my holster. I still didn't give the emergency code word because my boss knew that if I really thought I was in trouble, I would holler it out. He knew to stay where he was and keep observing and recording.

'Are you guys stupid? Do you really want to get busted? I said I'll meet you down the road.'

In that moment, I pulled myself back out of the car and started to walk. There was the sound of the car door shutting and then I saw them slowly cruise past me towards the end of the street. Suddenly the vehicle did a quick U-turn, came towards me, and then raced past. Something wasn't right. It looked like they'd twigged that they were caught up in police operation and were going to make a run for it.

The waiting unmarked police car did a U-turn and started to follow them as my boss's car screeched to a stop beside me. I jumped in and flicked on the lights and sirens. We were after them.

They were driving like lunatics, speeding down one-way streets, trying everything to shake us off. Finally they pulled over. The car had barely stopped before the doors were flung open and the guys were running in all directions. Everyone, that is, except the driver who managed to get stuck in his seatbelt and was still frantically trying to untangle himself as we ran up.

After the driver was arrested for a heap of offences, I checked out the back of the car. I found nunchucks[4], a baseball bat, rope, and a knife. I don't know what these guys had been planning to do that night, but it didn't look good. I was eternally grateful that they approached me and not a real street prostitute who could have been seriously assaulted, or killed.

---

4   A set of weapons consisting of two sticks connected by a chain or rope.

The very real possibility of those guys actually managing to pull me into their car, and then getting away, stayed with me for many months to come. I replayed the possibilities over and over in my mind. I had nightmares, and shook uncontrollably for weeks afterwards. I kept thinking about what would have happened if they had got me into their vehicle, and managed to get away from my boss and the other undercover cops. And when they found my gun and listening device, and worked out I was a cop, what then? Would they have let me go? Or hurt me? Or worse?

Say Cheese

'Only if you can promise me she'll never find out'

As emotions run raw in the divorce courts, money and assets are split in lawyers' offices, and children look on bewildered as their parents go in different directions, how many people involved in the breakdown of a relationship wonder how they possibly arrived at that point? What makes people run headlong into a potentially disastrous liaison? Why can't they read the signs from the onset? Or does it only all seem so obvious in retrospect? Were the danger signs there from the start, misinterpreted or ignored?

The good news is that in 2007, according to McCrindle Research, the number of marriages in Australia (116,322) was the highest in almost thirty years. On top of that, in the same year, divorces were down (47,963) to the lowest in twenty five years. But the divorce rate is still phenomenal. How many relationships start with one or both partners not entirely sure that it's going to work? And how many relationships start with distrust and suspicion?

In the US, prenuptial agreements are being embraced by more and more people. Initially, the process of deciding on the division of assets should a marriage fail before it was even initiated was viewed with horror. The proponents of the scheme maintained it was simply commonsense to safeguard against unreasonable distribution of wealth at the end of a short-term relationship. And the detractors vehemently pointed out that merely considering the prospect of a prenuptial agreement denied any faith in the relationship from the start.

Controversially, in many parts of the world private individual use lie detector (polygraph) tests to determine possible shortcomings in a relationship before committing to marriage. Not actually able to detect lies per se, the instrument records and measures responses like skin conductivity, body temperature, breathing, pulse and blood pressure while the subject is being questioned, and, depending on the interviewer's skill, these results may determine whether the subject is being deceptive or evasive in their responses.

In the early stages of some relationships, suspicion is the order of the day, and I am often called in to investigate every possible detail of a potential partner's background, particularly when large sums of money, businesses, and property could be at stake. My clients don't want to waste time cultivating a relationship that may be detrimental to them further down the track. These investigations may also reveal long forgotten indiscretions, depending on how far the client wants to go.

As a result of buying and selling well during the dot com boom days, Patrick is extremely wealthy. Now aged forty three, he's very good looking in a dark, Mediterranean way, with full, sensuous lips, huge languid brown eyes, and a body well acquainted to a regular gym routine. In every respect, he's a real catch. He's kind, generous, and intelligent, but he comes with a little bit of baggage.

Three years back, Patrick's thirty month marriage ended in an ugly and acrimonious divorce. After the messy settlement had been concluded, he found out that he'd been duped. His wife had been after his money from the start, and had been having an affair with her so-called ex boyfriend all along. It was generally accepted that she and the boyfriend had been working together over the whole thing and had taken Patrick for a ride. At the time, he hadn't the slightest suspicion of his wife's alter ego, and was deeply in love with her.

Now Patrick is more careful, often choosing to socialise with people who are unaware of the extent of his fortune, and who, he feels, take him for what he is, not for what he has. And it works. He isn't into a flamboyant lifestyle, so driving a nice but moderate BMW doesn't worry him. His apartment overlooking the river, which he vaguely refers to as being 'in the family', is very comfortable without being luxurious, and he prefers smart casual clothes over the number of Armani suits lurking in the back of his wardrobe.

Six months ago, Patrick met Katelyn at a dinner party, hitting it off straight away. His friend, Bruno, was always trying to get Patrick fixed up, inviting new women he thought he could introduce into Patrick's life to his parties. Patrick took all this with serene good-humour. After all, Bruno did have good taste, and Patrick would always end up having a good time, and, more often than not, become good friends with his arranged date. But, until Katelyn came along, that's all it ever amounted to – good friends.

That night, it was raining furiously. A deep depression was moving slowly down the south east coast, creating huge flooding in Brisbane. Patrick could hardly see through the windshield of his car as he parked outside Bruno's place, grabbed the two bottles of wine he'd brought, and bolted for the door. Head down, he didn't see a woman doing exactly the same from the opposite direction until they literally crashed into an embrace.

'Oh, god, I'm sorry,' she said. 'Have I hurt you?'

Patrick laughed. As they untangled themselves, he could smell fresh apple shampoo.

'I think I'm supposed to ask that,' he replied, pushing Bruno's door open with his foot. 'Going in?'

In the light, their eyes met. Patrick found himself tongue tied for the first time in many years. She was an extraordinary beauty, and he found himself being drawn, almost physically, towards her deep blue eyes. She brushed her long, blonde hair away from her face so that he could admire her high, Slavic cheekbones. She was laughing, no doubt at his gawping half-open mouth.

'Katelyn,' she said, thrusting her hand towards him.

Patrick closed his mouth and took her hand in his. He never wanted to let it go.

'I see you've met,' Bruno's voice boomed across the hall. 'Great night,' he added, ushering them through to the family room. Patrick looked back at him. Bruno winked through a grin that spread too far across his face to be considered decent.

If anyone was offended by Patrick's total focus on Katelyn that evening, nobody mentioned it. He cornered her at every possible opportunity, and she certainly seemed not to mind. She told him that she'd been overseas for some years, living in London, Chicago, and Rome, following a photographic career. She felt that she was now home for good. A relationship gone sour had been the impetus to return, and she was now, at twenty five, ready to settle and perhaps write.

They were soon meeting regularly, and within six weeks, sharing the same bed on a regular basis. From early on, Katelyn was clearly keen to initiate sex, but Patrick was more hesitant at first, wanting to be sure of the relationship. However, once over his concerns, he was delighted by Katelyn's enormous appetite for lovemaking, leaving him often utterly exhausted and very, very content.

He was so happy that he proposed to Katelyn two months later, suggesting a wedding sooner rather than later. It was planned for only twelve weeks down the track. On the guest list, Katelyn only had her parents to consider, and would bring them up from Melbourne, whereas Patrick's family all lived in Brisbane. Everything was set to go.

'But what do you really know about her, Patrick?'

John was Patrick's accountant, and had looked after his financial affairs with absolute wizardry for the fifteen years. It had been John who'd steered his battered finances back into shape after the collapse of his last marriage.

'She's caring, beautiful, and in love with me,' Patrick grinned back at him. 'What else would I need to know?'

'What she's been doing overseas? You can't tell me anything about that. You've had the wool pulled over your eyes once already. Don't let it happen again.'

They'd been over the same ground time and again over the last week. He totally understood John's concern, but he was starting to be a pain.

'At least let me organise some background checks on her,' John suggested. 'It'll be worth the money.'

'Now? This late? Two weeks before the wedding? Katelyn goes to Port Douglas with Jo, a girlfriend, for some R and R in three days time.'

'I shouldn't be telling you this,' said John, 'but another client of mine went lulu over a chick a few years ago. He'd been bitten in the bum over his previous marriage too, but there he was again, head-over-heels in love. You know something, Patrick? I didn't take to this girl from the moment I met her. She was furtive, sneaky, if you know what I mean.'

'And?'

'Well, this client was an old friend of mine. I suggested background checking and he hit the roof. He refused outright to have any checks done at all. But, days later, I took it on myself to do them anyway. I know, I know, it was wrong, and, believe me, I'd never do anything like that again. As it turned out, this girl was a hooker from Perth, and a mate of his ex wife. Nice work.'

'How did he feel about you doing the checks?'

'Oh, he fired me, and I deserved it. As a matter of fact, we're still good friends though, especially now he's with his current wife. The one he married after the Perth girl.'

Patrick sighed and hauled his long frame out of the chair.

'OK, if it makes you feel better, go ahead. I don't want you to stop being my accountant.'

'Anyway, why Port Douglas? Why are they going there?' John asked.

Patrick paused at the door.

'She's never been there, and wants to check out the Great Barrier Reef. I wouldn't mind going but I've got too much to do if I want to take Katelyn to Paris next month.'

'Who's keeping an eye on her up there?'

'What? John, c'mon she's a big girl ...'

John held up his hand.

'OK OK, it's just after the last time you told me never to let you do anything stupid again. And who is Jo anyway? What do you know about her?'

Patrick drove home in a thoughtful mood. Maybe he was being a bit one-eyed over John's concerns. He was only acting in Patrick's best interests. And what was the harm? And if Katelyn got a bit sozzled one night, so what? They'd done that together a couple of times. His mind drifted back to last week when they'd had a fair few glasses of bubbly. Katelyn had gone almost feral, tearing his clothes off and making love to him like a demented demon. Later, bruised and sated, she'd apologised for her roughness. 'Too much champagne does that to me,' she muttered, before falling asleep.

'What the hell!' Patrick pulled over, picked up his phone, and dialled his accountant's number.

'Organise Port Douglas, but only if you can promise me she'll never find out,' he told John. 'And not in her face either – she's supposed to be having a relaxing time.'

That's when John contacted me. We quickly got the background checking under way. John was a regular customer and knew what I needed. As he was giving me instructions for the Port Douglas gig, I was mentally running through my list of available agents. Three days of easy surveillance work at a five star luxury resort with all expenses paid. Swimming, shopping, fine dining, private spa, there was no choice here. I would have to do the job myself.

The weather was glorious when I checked into one of the best resorts I'd ever visited. Not wanting to be spotted on the same flight to Cairns, I'd arrived earlier than Katelyn and her friend. Lounging by the pool with a view of reception, I was already part of the furniture when they arrived. An hour later, they were sitting at a table five metres away from me, chatting and making short work of a bottle of Moet. This made things a lot easier. I did have a contact on the staff ready to let me know if they'd booked a tour or were intending to go shopping. My main concern was that they'd arrive and then scoot off somewhere else straight away. But, like most arrivals after travelling, the poolside was the order of the day.

They seemed very comfortable with each other, and it wasn't long before a fresh bottle of Moet was popped at the table. I settled back to read a magazine and listen to snippets of their conversations about fashion and gym work. Just as I was starting to feel guilty about my own lack of regular exercise, I heard a male voice and looked up.

Jo was on her feet with her arms around a real hunk of rippling muscle. A young, evenly tanned man with one of the most handsome faces in the resort. His companion, standing almost shyly to one side, was another superb physical specimen. I really have to get to the gym, I thought! Katelyn stood up as the boys were introduced as Andy and Bill. Bill was the shy one.

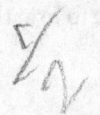

I watched as Jo's hands slid along Andy's sleek biceps as she talked. He seemed happy about Jo's attention, even slipping an arm across her shoulders and kissing the top of her head.

They all sat down, and with more Moet arriving, Katelyn became quite giggly. She was sculling it back at a fair pace, and hadn't eaten for a few hours as far as I knew. Suddenly, the conversation seemed to change from a light hearted chatter to a more sombre mood. I could see that Katelyn was weeping, her shoulders heaving with huge sobs. What was going on? I couldn't hear enough, catching only the odd word.

Jo, Andy and Bill all stood and helped Katelyn to her feet. She was very wobbly. Suddenly, as Katelyn's legs buckled, Bill reached out and scooped her into his arms, her head lolling heavily against his chest. She was completely drunk.

With all my gear ready, I was able to wander after the four of them as they headed back to the accommodation. I knew that Katelyn and Jo were in separate villas alongside each other and two down from mine. As I traipsed along behind, I saw something that changed the dynamics of the four people in front of me. Andy had his hand firmly on Bill's bum as they walked along, stroking his lower back from time to time. Not only that, the caressing was clearly in Jo's sight, and she was taking absolutely no notice of it. So the boys were gay. That was interesting.

I sat at the breakfast table outside my villa for a couple of hours with a glass of wine. Just on dinner time, the two boys emerged. They were laughing as they said goodbye to Jo at the door. She lifted a finger to her lips and glanced behind her into the room before kissing them both. As Andy and Bill left, I saw something that made me freeze. Andy was carrying a camera. Suddenly, I had a very unpleasant feeling about what was going on.

I called John immediately to tell him exactly what I'd seen, and, within four hours, both he and Patrick had chartered an aircraft and were meeting me in the reception foyer. We went through the surveillance videos together. Everything was there, including the number of times Jo and then the others had topped up Katelyn's drink. It was difficult to see if anything else had been added to her bubbly, but, considering her almost catatonic state as she was carried to the villa, it was highly likely.

My brief holiday was over. I returned to Brisbane the following day while Patrick and John confronted Jo. I heard later that Jo, knowing Katelyn's propensity for alcohol, and having an inkling of Patrick's enormous wealth, had admitted to contriving the whole amateur plan to blackmail her with photos of a supposed orgy. When Patrick confronted her, Jo might have been able to talk herself out of the situation, but on my suggestion, Patrick threatened to have the police involved if she didn't come clean straight away. He was prepared to forget the whole thing if she told the truth.

And how did Katelyn feel about being watched on holiday? How would you feel?

The Honey Trap

'He kept disappearing at parties. I should have seen the signs'

A large part of my work is finding out if partners are cheating. We call it integrity testing and, if it's done fairly, it's a sure-fire way of discovering if a partner has the tendency to stray. But we play fair to see if the partner will take the initiative when an opportunity presents, rather than have an agent make a full-on, sexually charged advance that blurs the line between tempter and tempted. And are there agencies out there prepared to go to almost any length to prove that a partner is prepared to stray? For sure, but I'd like to think that most agencies consider the consequences of their discoveries, and the total impact that they will have on a relationship. Mind you, by the time someone contacts me, they're already suspicious, so the relationship can be heading for the rocks anyway. Here's a typical case history:

In Brisbane, Jane, bright, intelligent and practical, is a receptionist in her mid-thirties, and has been married to John for four years. They don't have any children. John, almost forty, is doing well as a self-employed builder but has a few self-esteem issues. He's conscious of his age, his thinning hair, and that life's slipping by too quickly. Being overweight isn't helping.

They met at a party a year before they were married and simply got on well together. Nothing spectacular, she was looking for someone to settle down with, he made her laugh, she thought he was happy with her and their sex life, and that was enough for Jane.

Looking back, John's behaviour at parties should have rung some alarm bells. He would disappear for twenty to thirty minutes at a time and couldn't be found anywhere. At the time she never thought to ask him where he'd been. She assumed he was off having a laugh and beer with a mate somewhere. In those days he smoked a little marijuana, so he could have slipped away for a puff. Apart from that she had her own friends to chat to. Then, at one party not long before she contacted me, she found him with a very good friend of hers and was extremely unhappy with the circumstances.

It all happened quite quickly. Jane had remembered leaving her handbag down by the pool where they'd all been having something to eat earlier. It was quiet there, the lights were dimmed, and Jane made no sound. She was barefoot, having chucked her shoes into a corner to dance.

Thinking she was alone, Jane got a fright when she heard a chair scraping over the pool patio tiles. She froze, heart bumping, as she tried to peer through the dusk. She could just make out two figures standing together.

'Who's there?'

'Shit,' someone responded. She recognised the voice immediately. It was her husband.

Jane's voice tightened in her throat. She could smell perfume on the warm night air.

'John, is that you? What's going on?' she asked, squinting at the other person.

As her eyes adjusted to the darkness, Jane recognised Debbie standing next to her husband. She was surprised more than anything else. Debbie was her very best friend, all the way from high school days. And she'd been a bridesmaid at their wedding.

Jane spoke into the long, embarrassing silence.

'What's happening with you two?'

'Ask your fucking husband, Jane,' Debbie replied, pushing roughly past Jane and running up the steps to the house.

When confronted, John was very defensive, insisting that Debbie had come onto him. At the time, Jane took his word for it, cutting her best friend out of her life, even though they'd known each other for years and been very close. At first she felt betrayed by Debbie, but then started having doubts, asking herself where he'd been and who with, all the other times he'd been missing. That's when she emailed me.

By that time Jane was pretty certain that she wanted to find out how likely it was for John, given the right circumstances, to take advantage of a situation. She was quite clinical in her approach, supplying me with details of his business, car rego, hours of work, and photos. We discussed how best to approach him, whether to do it in a bar or through his business. Jane confidently told me the best way of contacting him would be as a customer. He was a pubby sort of bloke, and would be very comfortable meeting me in a hotel, as he did for many of his clients, and discussing a possible building job over a drink.

I gave John a call and told him I was from Darwin, staying in Brisbane while looking for a builder to start work on a new house on a block I had bought in Brisbane. Jane had told me that he'd never been to Darwin, so I was on safe ground. He was happy to meet me in a pub at 5.30 that afternoon, so I had to get some house plans together and find a suitable block to talk about so I looked genuine. I found what I needed and then added a few stains and scribbles to make them look well read. Everything has to be above suspicion, even clothing. Clients expect me to go off to meets in something ultra sexy, but that can inhibit and intimidate a man, and may look a bit over the top. Usually jeans and T shirts work best in these situations, the easily approachable, relaxed look.

This is where the job can become difficult, and it's not what I'm doing–I'm comfortable with that –it's how I'm doing it. I have to drink, or appear to, as much as possible, and that can be hard. I use every trick in the book to keep up without getting smashed. Drinking slowly, pouring drinks into pot plants if I have to, but I never leave my drink unguarded. A spiked drink can lead to all sorts of unexpected complications. Morally I'm happy to do this because I'm skilled at creating the social environment where it's up to the target to make the moves on me. I'm not leading him into temptation. He can discuss my building project in a social-professional sense over a drink, or he can recognise an opportunity and work towards that himself. I don't lead them on, or discourage them. They dig their own holes, or not, depending on what they want.

In this case it was a very long night. I had a hidden surveillance camera and was voice recording the conversation. There was also a male backup agent with nineteen years field experience watching me at all times, also video recording the situation. He was dressed like any bloke having a beer on a Friday night – very nondescript in appearance. He's mainly there in case anything goes wrong, and it can. Men with a few too many under their belts can get aggressive if they don't get what they want, so it's good to have that other agent around, but not in an obvious sense.

Over the first couple of hours I began to think John wasn't going to hit onto me. He was relaxed and enjoying himself, but wasn't making any moves to escalate the relationship. The only thing that kept me there was that every time I'd almost finished my beer he'd jump up to buy me another one, to the point where I'd had four and was feeling quite tipsy. Eventually he started to talk about his wife and his business, chopping and changing between the two. He asked me if I was single. When I told him I was, he asked me if I was happy. At this point I could feel a turnaround happening and he was about to make a move. This is the way the conversation went:

John: 'Are you currently seeing anyone?'

Me: 'No.'

John: 'Would you say that you're happy?'

Me: 'Oh, not really. I'm pretty lonely.'

John: 'Well, you seem like a nice person. You seem like you're a lot of fun.'

Me: 'Oh thanks.'

John: 'Yeah, it'd be nice to sort of catch up with you again another day, 'cause I'm not too happy in my marriage to be honest. I don't find my wife to be sexually attractive anymore. But I find you sexually attractive.'

Me: 'Really. Thank you.'

John: 'Can we meet up again another day, and can I ring you and email you?'

I gave him my decoy email and mobile number, and he bought another round of drinks.

John: 'My wife's not fun anymore. I'm looking for some fun in my life. I'm bored, and I love how you're giving me attention. I don't get that at home anymore.'

The attention aspect is important. Just listening, leaning forward with plenty of eye contact and the occasional sympathetic touch on the hand, builds relationships. Perhaps if more people appreciated this in their own relationships I wouldn't be so busy.

By this time, after six hours, I had to make a break. I'd already almost blown it when I stumbled over my name, nearly giving my real one. I told him I was hungry and had to eat, but he wanted to go with me. So there we were, heading for a noodle bar with my backup agent in tow. When we got there, John still wouldn't leave, even when I was served my food and began to eat. I put on a cranky tone and told him I wanted to eat alone and he could call me in the morning.

'Yeah, sorry, no problem,' he said, and tried to kiss me goodbye while I was eating my noodles.

Within an hour he was texting me: I want to see you now. I miss you already. Can I see you tomorrow morning? I'd told him I was staying at a hotel so then it was: Can I come to your hotel tonight? When I told him that he couldn't come to the hotel he asked if he could see me in the morning. When I said that he could meet me at 10am he begged to see me earlier at

8am and I agreed. I would meet him at the hotel I had told him I was staying at.

For two hours he continued to text me: I can't stop thinking about you. I really wish I was there with you right now.

I responded: Yeah, I wish I were with you too. Every time he sent a text I would respond with something like: Yeah, I feel the same way.

He was right on time the next morning and joined me at breakfast in the hotel. Now, this is an important part of the integrity test. Last night John would have happily followed me to my hotel for a romp. But sometimes a guy can get cold feet, even after all the passionate texting, and he may not show up the next morning. He may have second thoughts, and this can be important information for a client thinking about making life-changing decisions based on his behaviour.

The meeting in the hotel was video recorded by myself and my agent and voice recorded by me. No second thoughts for John. He drank a coffee while I had my breakfast, telling me he wanted to go up to my room with me. I told him I'd already checked out, and that I was off to the shops to buy a jumper. There was now sufficient evidence for the client, so I needed to shake John off. But as I went into the street, he stuck with me like glue.

John: 'Oh, can I come with you? I've actually cleared my morning to spend it with you. I cancelled my appointments.'

I couldn't get rid of him.

Me: 'Do you want another cup of coffee?'

John: 'Can you come back? Can I meet you? I'm going away on holidays with my wife and a couple of my friends, but when I get back I want to see you again. I want to take you away.'

Me: 'Sure, that'll be great. Look I really want to go shopping on my own.'

John got the picture and left, kissing me before he went. The operation was over. I had forwarded the text messages to Jane as they'd arrived, keeping her up to date with what had happened. All that was left was to forward her a transcript of the recordings, a DVD of the video work, and a report.

Most of my female clients want more details from an emotional perspective. Male clients are into the facts and don't want to know the nitty gritty like what I thought that facial expression meant, and what exactly she may have meant by a particular statement. Women take the whole thing apart for days, sometimes even longer, and clients often contact me way down the track to clarify something. Women generally want to make sure the decisions they make over what they've discovered are the right ones. Whether to forgive him, leave him, or ever trust him again, are issues for a woman, whereas men who discover their partners are cheating just want to get it sorted out and, usually, finished for good.

In Jane's case she took time reviewing the evidence and talking to me, and then rang to say that she realised John had been doing this a lot. She even reconciled with her friend, Debbie, telling her that she knew it wasn't her fault that John had started kissing her at the party. Debbie was able to tell Jane what had actually happened that night. John had asked her if he could have a quiet word. When Debbie asked him what it was about, John had indicated that he thought his marriage was heading towards rocky ground and he needed some advice. Once he had Debbie poolside, he tried to kiss her, and that's when Jane appeared.

On hearing that, Jane went through a period of self-doubt. Was it because she wasn't good enough in bed, wasn't pretty enough? It's hard to imagine what it feels like to have the person you love and trust say terrible things about your sexuality to another woman. Not long after the operation, Jane called to tell me that she'd packed all of John's belongings and left them on the front lawn. She'd kicked him out.

He was wild, more towards me than anyone else. He felt that I'd really taken him for a ride and he sent messages to his ex wife's mobile telling her he was out to get me. This happens quite often, and it's just part of the job. The guy's hormones were on a roll, then he's made to look like an absolute idiot – not good for a man's ego. I usually report people of concern to the police. They can have a chat and warn them off. That's usually all it takes, but it's always still in the back of my mind. After all, people can lose their jobs, relationships, homes and children over infidelity, sending them a bit crazy. And who's to blame? Not them, they think, so it must be me.

People have to be careful when they suspect that a partner's cheating in a relationship. When there's an inkling of suspicion it should just be noted, diarised if possible. There's no point going in all guns blazing because you'll most likely be deflected by a weak but possible excuse and only end up putting your partner on guard. Instead, quietly watch for giveaway behaviour: changes in routine; starting to take their mobile everywhere with them instead of being comfortable leaving it lying around; suddenly spending time on the computer late at night or early in the morning; last minute reasons to stay late at work, or unexpected weekend work and trips away; a new mate they keep dropping round to see, or go and have a beer with, or keep talking about. And they do keep talking about that 'new mate' because an illicit relationship is always top-of-the-mind.

People in illicit relationships always make mistakes, so look out for these. Credit card and mobile phone records are often a giveaway. Look for cash receipts for strange purchases or higher than normal mileages. Be on the alert for different body smells or perfumes. These kinds of things can begin to form a picture that leaves little doubt. Where there's smoke, there's usually an absolute blaze.

Close Call

'Drop the knife or I'll shoot!'

One night, not long after I'd left the prostitution unit, I was back in uniform patrolling New Farm in a marked police vehicle. I was back in general duties, and I had a new trainee with me, Dan. He had only just got out of the Police Academy a couple of weeks before. He was a little nervous, but keen and anxious to learn.

I had handed in my snub-nosed revolver that I'd worn in a thigh holster during my undercover work, and gone back to the regular issue .357 Smith and Wesson. I'd been trained on a .357 but hadn't been familiarised on, or fired, this particular firearm. I was due for some time in the range with it.

It was early in the morning and we were driving around the New Farm area. I was explaining my little rego plate obsession to Dan, telling him how successful it had been in identifying stolen vehicles. I was always at it, checking to see if both registration plates on a motor vehicle were identical. It was surprising how often they weren't – because it's difficult for crims to get hold of matching plates, the mismatch suggested that the vehicle was stolen or unregistered.

We were driving past the New Farm Library at about 2am, when I noticed a white van sitting alone in the library car park. My radar went off. I could see no good reason for that vehicle to be parked in the library car park after hours, so I had to check it out.

The parking area was bound on three sides by thick hedges with a small walkway through to the library building. To keep the suspect vehicle properly in view, I reversed into a car space opposite, and kept my headlights on. Dan used the radio to begin a registration check on the van's front plate while I walked over to the vehicle to check its rear one.

It turned out that both plates matched, and I was on my way back to the police vehicle when I heard a yapping sound coming from the van. I peered in through the firmly shut passenger window and saw a little Chihuahua jumping up and down on the seat, barking at me. I then noticed that the van's rear sliding door was slightly ajar. I remember thinking that where there is a dog, there's usually an owner not far away, and thought he must have gone for a walk somewhere.

Suddenly a long sabre blade flashed out through the gap in the sliding door, and sliced down past me. The knife came so close that I felt its breeze rough my hair.

I jumped back and screamed, 'It's the police! It's the police!'

The sliding door opened to reveal a wild-eyed man staring at me, his hair stuck up at all different angles. He jumped out of the van and started walking towards me, still holding the blade.

'Fuck off!' he screamed, still advancing towards me. 'Fuck off!'

'It's the police! I'm a cop. Drop the knife!' I yelled, as I started to back up away from him. I held the transmit button down on my radio microphone which I had attached to my right shoulder, and called to Police Communications for urgent assistance.

It wouldn't be long before the air would be split with screaming sirens and blue lights. All I had to do was keep the guy calm in the meantime. But something was wrong. I wasn't hearing any response from Communications. I kept repeating my request for urgent assistance, my voice sounding more and more panicked while I kept trying to keep my focus.

The wild-eyed man was still coming towards me yelling, 'Fuck off! Fuck off!' swinging the blade in an arc motion, back and forwards. He was trying to intimidate me, and it was working. I was terrified.

'OK, OK!' I shouted, backing away. 'Just put the knife down. Now!'

He kept advancing towards me, swinging the blade from side to side. Where was my backup? Why hadn't I heard from Communications? I should be hearing sirens by now.

Suddenly, to my horror, I found my back hard up against the hedge. I was trapped. He was still coming at me, madly swinging the blade. My mind went back to my firearms training – if you can't retreat from a life-threatening situation, shoot to kill. I realised, at that point, that I would have to take this person's life. I would have to shoot him. I felt sick.

I drew my gun from my holster and pointed it at the middle of his chest. I had my forefinger on the outside of the trigger guard. Just then, a figure appeared right in front of me. It was Dan. He'd completely forgotten the correct procedure when faced with a dangerous suspect. The idea is to form a triangle so that the suspect can't watch both officers at the same time, and here he was, standing between me and this man. Now my gun was pointing at my trainee's back.

'Get out of the fucking way!' I shouted. My adrenalin was by now so high, that I started to get tunnel vision[5]. This is where you can only see what's in front of you. It's a very weird sensation because even though you only notice what's in front of you, all your other senses are heightened.

Dan quickly moved further to the left and then drew his weapon.

---

5 In medical terms, tunnel vision is the loss of peripheral vision with retention of central vision, resulting in a constricted circular tunnel-like field of vision. Tunnel vision can be caused by extreme fear or distress, an intense physical fight, or intense anger, due to the body being rapidly flooded with adrenaline and oxygen. (source – Wikipedia)

I now had the man in my sights again, and he was still coming towards me swinging the blade. I moved my finger onto the trigger. This was his last chance. I started to break out in a sweat. I couldn't believe I was about to shoot someone. I hadn't felt so terrified in all my life. Not only was I feeling scared, but I was also very angry at this man for making me feel this way.

'Drop the knife now! It's the police! Drop it right now or I will shoot you!' I screamed as loud as I could. I could feel vomit making its way up into my mouth, and my hands started to shake.

He just screamed, 'I said fuck off!' at me again and took another step towards me. I squeezed the trigger on my gun as I stared right at his chest at where the bullet would enter. And the gun jammed.

At this point I knew I was about to die. It's funny the things that cross your mind when you think your life is about to end. I wondered how painful dying would be, and whether we really do go to heaven. I also thought about my new little kitten waiting at home for me, and about all the paperwork that would be involved in shooting someone, should I survive. Mortality is both horrifying and fascinating.

Somewhere in the freeze frame of all those thoughts, the man drew back his arm and threw the blade at me. It spun through the air as I ducked to the left. I saw it fly past my right shoulder and go straight into the hedge behind me.

Holstering my gun, I charged at him, giving it everything I had. Dan and I took him to the ground and handcuffed him. That's when I discovered that my radio button was in the off position. It had probably been knocked as I got out of the police vehicle.

Later, when the Inspector had arrived at the scene, I started writing my notes in my notebook. I was still so terrified that I couldn't write properly. And I had to write left-handed because my right hand, which had held the gun, shook the most.

Later, we ended up going to court where the man was found guilty of a few different offences. But to this day, I have never forgotten about making the decision to end someone's life. It is something that will stay with me forever.

Playing Fair

**'I reckon she's earning plenty,
and I'm the one paying.'**

Paying child support is part of the process of a relationship break-up. It's a necessary evil in a way, and there are plenty of people out there who think it's unfair. They're paying too much, not getting enough, or just getting screwed by the system and their ex's.

And then there are the people who find out that they've been channelling a huge proportion of their hard-won earnings into supporting their offspring in good faith, while the ex-partner has enjoyed another income stream. It's a surprisingly common situation, and very dangerous ground. In fact, the consequences can be catastrophic.

Mark, aged thirty four, is a self-employed Brisbane carpenter with a busy business built up through word-of-mouth. He's a trusting bloke, and although his marriage fell apart after only two years, he still feels deeply for his ex-wife, Emma.

They were living together for three years before they were married, and in that time had a daughter, now aged three. He's over the moon with that little girl and would do anything for her. He regrets not being able to spend more time than on weekends with her, but knows that until his business can support another carpenter, he's just going to have to keep up with the long hours to pay the hefty child support.

Emma's a friendly, gregarious woman, the sort who would cheerfully chat to her fellow passengers on a bus, or in the supermarket queue. Aged thirty, with immaculate skin, she's genuinely interested in health and beauty, having worked in the industry as a consultant for some years before becoming a mum. Like Mark, she feels the break up of their marriage was inevitable. They'd met on holiday, had a whirlwind romance, and ended up living together without too many things in common.

Mark believed that Emma, despite having a huge social network, was a stay-at-home mum, looking after their child in the best possible way. That was his understanding until a mate of his, Griff, gave him a call and told him that his girlfriend, Julie, was raving about Emma's business with a bunch of girls at a recent party. Mark's mate had hung around for a listen.

'It's all cash jobs,' Julie said, 'and she's busy day in and day out. She's making a fortune, but can't bloody well spend it.'

'What do you mean, can't spend it?'

'Well, what do you think? Her ex thinks she's not earning, so he's giving her heaps of dough for the kid and stuff. He's on a good wicket anyway. He's got his own business, and whenever she needs a bit extra he just hands it over.'

'Duh, she'd be really smart driving around in a new car when she's on child support then, wouldn't she?'

'Too right, that's why she's got to spend it on things that aren't obvious.'

Griff was tempted to have a go. He was disappointed in his girlfriend's attitude. It made him think twice about where they were at too. He waited a bit longer, but the conversation moved on to other things. He felt sorry for Mark. He worked bloody hard and always trusted everyone to do the right thing.

'Mate, it's pretty rude,' Griff told Mark over the phone. 'I was ready to get stuck into the greedy bags, but luckily I was driving that night, so I was sober and didn't go shooting my mouth off like I usually do. I thought you could maybe do something about it.'

Mark, stuck in gridlocked traffic on Samford Road on his way to another late night job, fumed when he thought about the money he was paying and the long hours he was working. As he sat drumming his fingers on the steering wheel, he happened to look up. Right in his line of sight was a billboard I'd had recently erected, and it just so happened to refer to child support payments. I don't know anyone who could possibly have ignored that sort of timely sign, and Mark certainly didn't. Blessing the foul traffic for once, he was straight onto the phone and speaking to me. By the time he'd cleared the gridlock, I'd made most of the arrangements to help him out.

One of my agents, Thea, would have to be a customer at Emma's home-based salon. We used Emma's mobile, presuming that would be the number she would use for her business. When Thea called, it was simple. Thea mentioned a friend of a friend in a chatty, bubbly sort of way, and, in no time, she was booked for a facial. Thea's great like that. She can burble away at nothing when in fact her mind's razor sharp, looking for ways to steer a conversation and extract information.

So Thea trots off to the beauty salon, telling me she thinks it's a great way to earn a living while I slog over the accounts. She's dressed in designer jeans and a lovely yellow top, and her story is that she's a shift worker in a call centre with time off during the day.

Thea has actually done call centre work. It's critical to get the cover story right before starting an op because agents have bummed out too easily through lack of preparation, or not thinking quickly enough on their feet. Creating and being totally familiar with a new identity gives an agent the power of confidence, so instead of worrying about their cover, they're working on the information gathering. To do this, it's best to have elements of truth in the cover story, like where the agent lived at one time, or the sort of work they did. It's disastrous to claim to have worked in a chicken soup factory and then be faced with having to talk to someone who owns one.

Thea came back from Emma's salon relaxed and with glowing skin. And she'd got the goods. The salon had three customers that morning, including Thea, and it was a gabfest. Emma was excited. She'd become so busy she'd taken a friend on as an assistant. The friend was a manicurist and was keen to join Emma, preferring to work for cash under the table. As Thea stealthily recorded with covert video and audio surveillance, Emma chatted about a holiday she and her daughter were planning. It was the second one up north at an upmarket resort this year. They all conferred over the clothes she'd need to buy, and some of the tourist spots they were thinking about visiting.

'I'm thinking of hiring a really nice car this time,' Emma commented, 'but I don't want to use a credit card. I don't think they do cash only.'

'My credit card wouldn't be any use to anyone. It's completely maxed,' Thea remarked.

'Oh, I pay cash for everything I can. It's the only way to go, no paper trails!'

The girls all laughed.

'Half your luck,' Thea said, forking out the cash for her facial. Needless to say, she didn't ask for a receipt.

Mark wasn't very happy with the news. I could tell from his voice that he would have preferred to hear that Emma was doing only occasional work for a couple of bucks here and there, not operating a full-time business. It was time for him to hand over all the information to the Child Support Agency.

Emma was extremely fortunate, receiving only a severe warning. However, she did have to pay assessed taxes on her prior earnings, which meant no luxury holidays for a while. It could have been more serious. Tax avoidance is a criminal offence, and obtaining child support income under false pretences is fraud. Rorting the system is tempting and seems like easy money. But when someone else's pocket is being affected, as Mark's was, it becomes very difficult to keep a secret.

Mark's financial burden was considerably eased, but the relationship with Emma took a long time to recover. Mark was disappointed and hurt that Emma could have taken him for a ride, and Emma felt betrayed when Mark informed the CSA.

There's no doubt that thousands of people are rorting the system, and a great percentage get away with it for years. But that's where a cheat can dig a hole for themselves, because once the rort is discovered, the CSA and ATO can go back a long way for their assessments, meaning repayments of thousands of dollars, prison, or a criminal conviction. And it's no good being in cahoots with the ex. It doesn't take much to fall out over something, and then it's all on. And once a person has fallen foul of a government department, that's it, they're marked for life.

A Double Life

'She doesn't answer her mobile?'

Sometimes people jump to the wrong conclusions, and in Daniel's situation that was certainly the case. He and his wife, Alison, were living in Townsville. They'd been married for eight years with two children in primary school and, according to everyone who knew them, they were reasonably happy.

Alison, a beautiful and striking brunette with huge liquid eyes, high Slavic cheekbones, and perfect figure, has a bubbly personality and can hold an intelligent conversation. She was a high-powered PA before marriage and the children came along, and that's how she met Daniel.

Tanned and trim, he was incredibly good-looking, dressing to kill in designer everything. He was immaculate, spending bucket loads of money on his wardrobe, knowing that in the high-end business dealings he was involved in, looking great counted. He openly bragged that he really enjoyed spending money on himself.

And that was the rub in their relationship. As soon as Alison gave up work and he became the sole earner, he restricted her access to money so that she had to ask for every cent and justify all her spending. And for a woman who was unused to looking anything less than her best, this was a dreadful predicament. As clothes and accessories became worn out or horribly out-of-vogue, her self-esteem crumbled. Over the years, she began to act as dowdy as she felt.

Daniel rang me because he felt that something wasn't quite right, and he had to get to the bottom of it. At first he was very curt, asking to be put through to the managing director of the company. He was incredulous that I, a female, was the managing director, and that I owned the business. He even openly questioned that a woman could own and run a PI company, and, at first, was extremely reluctant to deal with me.

Once we'd broken the ice, his concerns flooded out. Was it possible his wife was having an affair? There wasn't much for him to go on, but he was having difficulty contacting her on the few occasions that he called her during the day. Her mobile was always switched off, and while he assumed that she was just out having coffee with her friends, she still didn't return his calls for hours.

Over recent months, she'd started to look better too, more cheerful, as if something exciting was happening in her life. Clothes began to appear that he was sure he hadn't seen before. When he questioned her, she laughed at him, telling him that these were old numbers, and that fashions swung around again after a few years.

Daniel gave me everything I needed – recent photo, car rego, addresses, and we started surveillance on the following Monday.

In the morning, Alison, dressed in jeans and a simple floral blouse, left home with her children and drove them to school, dropping them off at the gates. My agent, Tania, and I looked at each other. Where was it to be? Up until this point everything had been predictable – kids, school, now it could be anything. Tania and I could be shacked up together in a stinking hot car for a few hours, grabbing coffee and some unhealthy munchies on the run, or we could be traipsing through designer shops as our target spent a leisurely day checking out the fashions. It was going to be a roaster, the temperature was already a muggy 30 degrees, so we both prayed for retail therapy.

Alison did a U turn in the car and headed towards town. It looked very much like we'd soon be enjoying some air-conditioning. But you never can tell.

A major part of our work is watching people. That's what we do. And if there's an exciting aspect of the job it's right when I have no idea where I'm going, or what's going to happen. That's when a PI relies on his or her skills. We have to keep close, yet out of sight. We have to blend. There's no point trailing someone into an upmarket restaurant dressed like a bum. You've got to have some idea of style and be ready to do a quick change in the car if you have to.

Alison continued through town, past all the major stores, and went down to the bay, pulling up outside a café. This was interesting, perhaps a meeting? When she sat at a table outside, the staff brought her a coffee and a muffin without taking her order. She was obviously a regular, and alone. I looked longingly at the coffee and reached for the vacuum flask. A decent cuppa would come later.

As we scrunched down in our seats trying to avoid the sun streaming through the open windows, Alison sipped her coffee and read her magazine. She didn't look or glance around her, clearly not expecting anyone to join her. At 9.30am she yawned, put on her sunnies, gave the waiter some cash and went back to her car. Gratefully winding up the air-conditioning, we pulled in behind her at a safe distance and followed.

Her next move really surprised us. We're not supposed to have preconceived impressions of people, but anticipating someone's intentions does help. It's a gut instinct sometimes and usually reliable.

Alison drove into the gated staff parking area at the back of a brothel. I assumed she was shopping in the area and had either parked there inadvertently, or knew it was one of those handy spots most people know of in our own towns. But she then did something completely unexpected. In a brisk, matter-of-fact manner, she locked the car and went up the back stairs into the brothel's staff entrance.

For a full thirty seconds, Tania and I said nothing.

'Did you see that?' Tania asked.

'I did. Did you get it on video?'

'Absolutely, do you think she'll be out in a minute? What the hell's she gone in there for anyway?'

I thought for a moment about Daniel's remarks about her clothes and her newfound happiness.

'I don't think so,' I murmured, making some notes. 'I think we may be here for a few hours.'

Certainly plenty of women work as prostitutes, even when they're married or in a relationship. But Alison didn't fit the stereotype at all. There are always surprises in this work.

And I was right about the hours. We waited. Alison didn't reappear until 2pm when she casually stepped into her car. Our suspicions, although clear enough, had to be verified, so while Tania hopped out to confirm she'd been working as a prostitute and not just paying a social visit, I followed Alison while she drove around to pick up the kids from school. Tania would stick her head in the brothel door, pretending to be a friend of Alison's running late to meet her. That conversation opener would be all it took for Tania to get the information we needed.

The only thing different about Alison when she came out of the brothel was that she was wearing a plain white blouse.

I figured she would have either taken it in with her or kept it there with her working outfit, so that she could change after a shower. I also worked out that she would have earned a possible $1,000 in that time, which was probably safely in a bank account her husband had no idea existed. Not bad for four hours work.

Of course, her prostitution earnings are taxed with everything legal and above board. The days of sleazy fleshpots are pretty much over. A few years ago, an escort was pretty much that, companionship mostly with a little negotiating for sex on the side. Now an escort is a prostitute, it's a career, a profession, it's legal, and much, much safer for the girls too.

I called Daniel to give him my report as soon as Alison had picked the kids up from school and returned home. When I told him what we'd seen, there was a sick silence while he regained his composure over the phone. I could tell that this had hit him very hard. I'm sure that he would much rather have heard that his wife was enjoying an illicit affair during the day than working in a brothel. He would have been able to handle that better, because that's what he expected to hear. He then pulled down the mental shutters on me.

'Just send me everything you have, video footage, details, OK?' And then he hung up.

Daniel initiated immediate separation and divorce proceedings. He felt outraged and because of his wife's work went for total custody of the children. But the courts don't regard a person's professional status as grounds for questions of custody. Alison wasn't doing anything illegal, no laws were broken, the children's health or well-being wasn't compromised, and she was paying her taxes. He was stumped.

Prostitutes are no different to anyone else. They're normal people with work to go to and a job to do. Top-of-the-line ladies can earn well over $1,000 an hour, but they've usually got a magazine or show profile. Some students pay their way through Uni by prostitution. Other people will go for it for a couple of years to earn the deposit for a house. It's a day's work, that's all. Like most people, they get into a different headspace and off they go. But it's certainly not work that suits everyone. And it's not the sort of profession you chat about over a glass of wine at your husband's work dinner. Prostitutes walk a very thin line and have to keep their work and private lives completely separate.

It's not always easy street – far from it. Many sex workers come from troubled backgrounds. Quite often it's a history of sexual abuse, and working in the sex industry only creates more psychological problems, often resulting in drug dependence. That's when the downward spiral starts. Looks and health deteriorate as earnings feed the habit, and before long the worker is virtually unemployed, often homeless, and living in abject poverty as they roam the streets offering cut price oral sex and back alley gratification.

On the streetwalker level, the work is far more dangerous. Let's face it, the very act of voluntarily jumping into a complete stranger's vehicle lifts the risk to another level. Some punters aren't satisfied with quick sex in the back seat. They may have another, far more sinister, agenda, with a vicious beating or killing planned.

Streetwalking is also illegal, so there's always the chance of arrest, a fine, or imprisonment. And then there are the pimps. With a total lack of empathy, these people offer protection for a hefty slice of the night's takings, supply the drugs to keep workers in a permanent state of need, and don't hesitate to hand out severe punishment for the slightest perceived 'offence' such as lack of productivity, or understatement of earnings.

Alison was fortunate. She moved on, finding she didn't need that sort of work after separating with Daniel. It had worked for her, and she got what she wanted out of it, emerging unscathed.

Is Death a Permanent State?

'There's a bad smell coming from the room'

During a particularly boring day shift, my partner, Phil, and I were driving around in our patrol car when we were advised to attend a men's hostel in Spring Hill. The manager had called the police because he hadn't seen one of his borders for quite a while. In fact, quite a few days, and he could smell something very bad coming from the man's room.

We looked at each other. Nothing was said, and we didn't need to say a word. We both had exactly the same thought about what we'd find. And it wasn't anything good.

The manager took us to the room, and, before we'd even arrived at the door, we could smell something terrible wafting down the hallway. We looked at each, again wordlessly. The smell of a dead, putrefying body is something never forgotten. It's a thick, cloying smell that seems to get everywhere and stick.

'Do you have the keys?' I asked the manager.

'No, I can't find them.'

We needed to get into that room, and quickly. Our observations aside, there was a remote chance the man might still be alive. If he was, and smelt like that, he would need very urgent attention.

Phil was particularly good at kicking down doors, so we stood back while he gave it one swift, deadly boot. As it banged open, the smell hit us like a thick cloud. I could almost feel the rotting flesh swirling around us, suspended in the room, and had to turn my head away for a breath of cleaner air before going in.

Lying face down and naked on the kitchenette floor was a man. He was very still, so the first thing I did was rush over to check for any signs of life. It didn't look good. I flicked cockroaches off his back and could see where they'd been nibbling at his flesh as I searched for a pulse in his neck. There was nothing there, and he felt stiff and cold. I was careful not to lean into a pool of liquid around his body as I checked further. That's when I saw that his blood had drained to the bottom of his body towards his chest and stomach, a common occurrence after death when a body hasn't been moved.

I asked Phil to go to the police car and radio for an undertaker to remove the body while I looked around the room for something to identify him. I was also hoping for some information to help locate a family member, so I could let them know he'd died.

I'd just started searching through the drawer of a little duchess and had found a name amongst a heap of paperwork when I heard a loud groan. In the deathly quiet of that room it came as a shock, and I must admit I screamed out loud, dropped the paperwork, and spun around quickly, scared stiff at what I'd see. The guy's fingers were moving. He was still alive.

Darting over, I knelt beside him.

'It's the police. It's OK. We're here. We're here. Stay with me.'

He groaned again, and then went quiet. I started stroking the top of his shoulder blade so he could feel that he wasn't alone.

'I need an ambulance!' I shouted, as loud as I could.

The manager ran into the room and went horribly pasty-faced when he saw what was happening.

'Call triple-o and get an ambulance here now. He's still alive!'

As the manager rushed out of the room to make the call, Phil wandered back in.

'Quick!' I urged. 'Go back down to the car and cancel the undertaker and request an ambulance. This guy is still alive. Let the hospital know he's on his way in too.'

I stayed with the guy, just stroking him and begging him to hang on. I stared around his tiny little room and felt terribly sad. There was one mug, one plate, one bowl, and pitifully few belongings. What a lonely life he must have had. And no-one had realised he'd been out of the loop until they'd smelt that something was wrong. How long had he lain there, on the cold floor, wondering when he'd be rescued, if ever?

Incredibly, he made a full recovery. It seems that our 'dead' man had fallen, hitting his head on the corner of the table. He'd then slipped in and out of consciousness as the days went by and, without food or water, gradually deteriorated to a near death state.

It made me begin to think about people looking out for each other, and how it happened less these days. I was only with that guy for a very short time before the ambulance arrived, but it really impacted on my own life and my attitude towards others. I started to appreciate my neighbours more, asking after them and friends when I hadn't seen them around. A quick phone call, or even a text message, works wonders.

At the end of the day, if we're not here for the purpose of being with and helping others, then what's the point? To me, the entire meaning of life is our relationship with other people.

Nappy Rash

'I don't know what's happening to my children'

It's probably a parent's worst fear to think that their child isn't being looked after properly. And during separation proceedings emotions always run high, as financial matters, accusations, and child custody claims are noisily aired. Where love, respect and kindness once existed, they're often replaced by hatred, contempt, and a need for revenge. Right in the middle of this are the children, battered from pillar to post as their parents fight it out, often used as trading tools to gain leverage, and always at the emotional sharp end of any disagreement.

In most cases, everything eventually calms down as the parents' lives adjust to different directions. New horizons open up, sometimes for a better life, new partners offer exciting possibilities, and a change of perspective is often a very good thing for everyone. Or is it?

What about the kids, where do they fit in? Who has them when, and is it convenient? How do they work in a new relationship? What's happening to them? They come back different, acting strangely. Maybe they're subdued, hurt, wild, disobedient, or foul-mouthed. Or perhaps no-one gives a damn about them because they're a pain in the backside.

In Gladstone, Isabella and Craig are in their mid-thirties, separated from each other, and with a three-year-old son and a one-year-old daughter. They married when they were both twenty eight, after living together for a couple of years. They met when Craig was a bit wild, and that's what attracted her to him. He quite liked her motherly, grown up ways. She calmed him down a bit, made him think about responsibilities – for a while, at least.

A hard-working brickie, Craig didn't take too well to being a dad. Looking after kids took him away from his mates, got in the way of his relaxation time with a few beers and his precious footy at the end of a tough day. And he wasn't really concerned how Isabella managed her day, that's what women do, it's their job, and they should just get on with it. Blokes had work to do, and women looked after the rest.

Isabella was a doting, caring mother who lived for her children. She was intensely protective, never letting them out of her sight for more than a few moments.

One night, Craig was at his local having a few beers after work. Usually the last thing on his mind was Isabella and the kids, but he was still simmering over the row he'd had with his wife that morning.

'You're a bloody irresponsible shit,' she'd told him, yelled at him, more like.

Craig sipped his beer morosely. It wasn't enough to be going out working long hours in all sorts of shitty weather. He was supposed to be home early to look after the bloody kids while she went out with her mother. What was she doing all day? What does she need to go out at night for? And was it his fault that he was playing pool and forgot? You can't just leave in the middle of a game.

The pub was quiet for a Thursday, and probably just as well. Craig didn't feel up to drinking with the usual blokes. It would slow down his drinking.

'Hey Craigie, coming out for a smoke?'

It was Angela, the sister of one of Craig's footy mates. She was a wild sort, always on the lookout for something different to do. The last time Craig saw her was in the back seat of a car with her legs wrapped around the driver's neck. She'd chucked her undies out of the window at him as the car raced off to a late night party somewhere. She was a good laugh alright.

Craig and Angela took their beers outside into the smoking pen.

'Gives you the shits not being able to smoke inside anymore,' Angela said. 'Look at this, will you? It makes you feel like you're diseased.'

'Still got your knickers from the other night, Angie,' Craig said, nudging her, 'under the front seat of the ute.'

Angela laughed. Craig thought she had a sexy laugh, and liked the way she put her hand on his thigh to steady herself on her stool.

'Maybe you should put them back on later, Craigie,' Angela whispered, leaning into his leg.

Craig's blood began to pound in his chest. This was too easy. He'd always fancied Angie, but whenever he'd made a move on her at a party she'd always brushed him off with the 'you're married' bit.

They talked and drank on that night. Craig was careful not to talk about Isabella and the kids, keeping the conversation light and easy. That wasn't too hard with Angie, she was a fun-time girl, not really interested in other people's issues, and that suited Craig fine. He was sick of talking about stuff at home, kids' clothes, food budgets, all too much of a drag. He was only young once and wanted to make the most of it.

Half a dozen people saw Angela slide into the front seat of Craig's ute that night. They were both well over the limit, but that wasn't about to worry either of them. They had other things on their minds.

When Isabella found out, she immediately moved back to her parents' place with the children. And, within days, Angela had moved into the home Isabella had once shared with her husband. It was full-on party time.

At first, Craig had little or nothing to do with his two children, seeing them from time on a weekend. And then he realised that he could reduce the amount of his child maintenance payments by having them for longer. He told Isabella that Angela had moved out, he missed his kids, and wanted to see more of them. He started by taking care of the children for four hours every Saturday and Sunday, intending to increase the frequency a few weeks down the track.

To Isabella, there was nothing untoward about Craig's change of attitude. He was the kids' father, he was becoming more responsible, and it was natural for him to want more time with them. She had no idea that his motives were more financial than fatherly.

After the first weekend, Isabella felt slightly uneasy. On both days the children had been returned grubby, and the three-year-old, Seth, complained of being hungry. When she questioned Craig about it, he shrugged her off.

'Kids are kids. They get dirty when they're having a good time.'

'But you can at least change her nappy. I'll give you some clean ones.'

Isabella began to think things weren't right when Seth came home the following weekend and told her that a lady had played with him. And the baby, Ava, had come back fretful. Isabella had prepared a bottle for her and it hadn't been touched. She'd also come back wearing a very dirty nappy even though Isabella had supplied spare ones that were returned unused. Painful rashes and sores were appearing around Ava's bottom half, and that was something she'd never suffered before.

Isabella became more concerned when Ava started vomiting and running a temperature whenever she'd been at her father's place. That's when she contacted me. If, as she suspected, the kids weren't being looked after, she wanted to prove it so she could restrict the time they had with Craig and make sure they didn't come to harm.

The thing with this kind of case is that unless we have access to the house and the opportunity to record what's happening indoors, proving neglect is difficult. All I can do is set up a surveillance operation and report back to the client. In this case, we immediately discovered that Angela was still in the picture, coming, going, and spending nights there, proving that Craig was lying. We followed Angela to her workplace, obtaining video and still footage so that Isabella could identify her. It was possible that, later down the track, if the relationship between this woman and Craig soured, she could supply information to Isabella about the way the kids had been treated.

This sort of surveillance is easy. Angela was not in the least bit suspicious that anyone was following her. Why would she be? She'd done nothing wrong. She left for work bang on eight and drove to an insurance office. She even worked at a desk in full view of the street. Interestingly, she was extremely cosy with a colleague over lunch in the café, something Craig wouldn't have been too impressed with. But we weren't working for him.

We got lucky in one instance when Craig took the kids to the park. Within minutes two of his mates arrived with an esky full of beer and didn't leave until it was finished three hours later. During that entire time Craig appeared to be totally oblivious to the fact his children were there with him. At one point, Seth was chugging beer from some of the stubbies lying around. It went unnoticed. When his friends left, Craig fell asleep on the grass. He didn't feed either of the children, or change the baby's nappy, even though he'd been there for almost four hours. He didn't wake up until the baby had been crying for ages – it was heartbreaking watching, but it was excellent video evidence for Isabella.

I taught Isabella how to gather more evidence by diarising the kids' visits to their father, taking photos of secretly marked nappies before and after to show that they hadn't been changed, marking levels on feed bottles to show they hadn't been used. She kept doctors' reports and recorded any illnesses, took photos of chaffing and ulcers. Of course, all this had to be done secretly. If Craig had known that Isabella was onto him he would have changed his behaviour. And that's not to say improve it – he was too much into his own scene for that. Isabella had already pleaded with him to look after the kids better, but he really didn't care less.

The sad fact is that without any hard evidence it's all circumstantial. The gathered information can only paint a picture of what's happening, rather than prove it outright. And, yes, being a mum makes me extremely sympathetic. I'd go crazy if I thought my girls were being mistreated in any way, especially if I couldn't get near them. It would tear my heart out, so I can understand a parent's intense emotional reactions. And sometimes there's nowhere for them to go for advice. The social services are under-resourced, the police have their hands tied, and most private investigation companies know how difficult it is to get proof so they keep clear of these cases.

And how did this particular case end? Isabella was able to confront Craig with a heap of facts, most of which she'd gathered on my advice, plus the video footage. He was stunned. She told him that she still had feelings for him and was prepared not to take it any further if he gave up having the children. He backed off straight away, and, to this day, he sees virtually nothing of his kids, except for the occasional visit.

Dark Shadows in Cyber Space

'All my friends turned against me.'

Only a few years ago, social interaction was limited to face-to-face physical meetings, the post, or using an intermediary like the letters to the editor page in a newspaper. The mail was one of the most important functions of a civilised country, linking businesses and people in a system that was thousands of years old. The only difference between the missives of the Roman Empire to its far flung protectorates and a postcard from Uncle Joe in Rome to his nephew in Sydney was speed. What took months, if not years, in 199 AD, took a matter of a few days in 1999.

But then, as the internet came into its own, everything exploded. Right now we can tap away at our keyboards discussing matters with hundreds, if not thousands, of people simultaneously, even see them on webcams, or talk to them on VoIP[6]. Suddenly our perception of socially interacting with people takes on new meaning now that relationships can be formed and maintained solely in cyberspace.

There are hundreds of social networking websites, and the number is growing every day. On top of that, there are thousands of chat rooms where rapid typing covers everything from knitting (yes, people still do that) to explicit sex. In both pastimes there's a niche for everyone and every taste. It's sometimes just a matter of finding the right chat room. Stumbling into the wrong ones can be extremely interesting.

With the internet comes another social phenomenon – anonymity. The 'Anon' label was once the domain of those writers who wished to disguise their true identities, and benefactors who preferred not to advertise their generosity or affiliations. Today millions of internet users have the opportunity to contrive or adopt a different persona to their own. And with that comes a new confidence.

How often are comments made over the internet, in chat rooms, forums, or in emails, that definitely wouldn't be made to another person face-to-face? When a person hides behind a false identity, are there any limits to how far they can go in insulting another? Can anything be done to stop them? We live in the world of the instant celebrity, a world where bad behaviour is often encouraged and traded for a moment of

---

6   VoIP – Voice over Internet Protocol or internet telephony.

fame. But what about people on the receiving end of bad behaviour, the victims, especially in the anonymous world of cyberspace?

Carol is a data processor, married for ten years with three children at school. Her husband, Pete, is a mechanic with his own steady business, so they don't have any financial worries. For Carol, her marriage is picture-perfect. She loves her home, her family life and Pete to pieces.

Everything in Carol's life is just right except for one thing. She's acutely conscious of being overweight. Pete calls it cuddly, telling her that he adores her 'roly poly bits'. He always says that he finds her sexy, and she knows that he means it. But, ever since she had the children, she's never been able to shake off the flab from around her tummy. She's tried every diet under the sun, even going to the gym which she hated, feeling that everyone was laughing at her.

Pete and Carol's social life outside the home is limited to chasing around with the kids' school and sports activities. This suits Carol. She feels uncomfortable going anywhere different from the day-to-day places she has to take the children, or the local shopping centre. Her work is now mostly done from home, which means not having to squeeze into tight, ill-fitting clothing all week. The less she has to go out, the better.

Anyway, Carol has all the social life she can handle. A couple of years back a friend, Amy, gave her a peek into the world of chat rooms on the internet. To begin with, Carol was totally bamboozled by the concept of meeting a hundred or so people in a virtual room and joining conversations. How could anyone keep up with the stream of unintelligible chatter typed at speed and pouring out fast onto the screen in front of their eyes? Carol was used to emailing in whole sentences with reasonably correct grammar and plenty of time to consider an answer. This in-the-moment chat room stuff was horrendous.

Over a couple of hours, and with Amy's help, it all began to make more sense. Obviously in the chat room that Amy used, many people knew each other and some had been chatting for months, if not years. Some had the weirdest usernames, but they all made Carol welcome, allowing her time to feel her way around and make silly newbie mistakes. The great thing was that she could already type extremely quickly. All she had to do was get the lingo.

Within a week, Carol felt completely at home in her chat room and had ventured into a dozen others. She initially recoiled from some, shocked at the strongly suggestive language. Later she would creep back to watch quietly as one person would explain what they would do to another in very sexually explicit terms. It was like looking through someone's bedroom window in a sense, although this way she wouldn't get caught.

Pete never got it. He had a look over her shoulder one evening, impressed as she chatted to eight people at the same time, but soon lost interest when his beloved motor racing came on TV. Pete, conscious of his wife's battle with her weight, was pleased she'd found something to interest her in the evenings. He was even happy to listen to her nightly reports of the activities of others, asking after this person or that from time to time.

For Carol, this was the perfect social life. With her extended family she could be as funny, silly, or risqué as she chose, depending on which chat room she was in. And it didn't matter what she looked like. Sometimes she altered her username to suit a different personality, or the mood she was in, and had a great time teasing the odd man here and there just for fun. Well, she assumed they were men, you never could tell really.

Over a couple of years, Carol developed strong on-line relationships, based on an element of trust, with some of the folk she had met in the first chat rooms she had visited. They knew her well, as she did them. She could be open and honest, appreciating the shared candour of their lives. And share they did. Opinions, photos, jokes all flittered through the ethernet, giving substance to the people behind the keyboards.

Dan got on well with Carol. He appealed to her sense of humour, and she responded to his funny lines with clever remarks of her own. They would often be the only ones left nattering away in the room when the others had long gone to their beds. They both found this hilarious. When Dan's wife left him, Carol was particularly sympathetic, often spending hours with him in the private chat rooms as he poured out his sadness and anger. As the confidences flowed between them, so did further details of their personal lives. Carol lived in Brisbane, Dan in Adelaide. She told him about her battles with her weight and how the chat rooms had eased that discomfort. One night, Dan asked her if they could meet if he came to Brisbane. He wanted to take her out for a glass of wine, just to thank her for her kindness.

Carol's fingers hesitated over the keyboard for the very first time. She wasn't sure what to say. Meeting Dan was out of the question. She was more than happy with their chat room relationship, it meant everything to her. But meeting up was something entirely different. That would change everything, especially after some of the quite intimate discussions they'd had. If it was one of the other women it would be OK. But not a man. Not Dan, anyway. How could she tell him, without upsetting him? He was so sensitive.

Words tapped across her screen.

'Are you there?'

She responded.

'Sorry, spilt my coffee, mopping up.'

Carol kicked herself. Dan knew that she never drank coffee this late at night. They'd had that discussion last week.

More words.

'I'm disappointed if you have to think about this.'

'I don't know,' she typed back, 'it doesn't feel right. We've got a wonderful thing going on-line. Why can't we just keep it at that?'

This time Carol waited, and waited. Dan's next words shocked her.

'Maybe it's not enough for me, and I know you feel the same. We can spend the night together and talk about it.'

Carol's hands flew across her keyboard.

'Dan, you've got the wrong idea. I'm totally happy with my life. I love Pete, you know that. I've told you a thousand times how much my kids and home mean to me. I don't want to spoil what you and I have. Let's forget about all this and go back to where we were.'

Again Carol waited. A few minutes later she saw Dan's ID exit the chat room. He had gone without replying or even saying goodnight. She was devastated.

Over the following week, Dan didn't appear in the chat room at all. All the regulars asked after him while Carol stayed quietly in the background. There was no way she could tell them what had happened. And, anyway, Carol was beginning to wonder if some of this was her fault. Had she led Dan on somehow? She knew she was sometimes cheeky on-line, so might that have been misinterpreted?

When Dan came back, she was relieved at first. He slipped into the chat room one Wednesday evening saying he'd been away on business unexpectedly with no internet connection available. But, by Friday night, she wished he'd never reappeared. Apart from completely ignoring her when she commented on something he said, he began to make snide comments about her, or would leave the chat room when she entered.

At the same time, two people joined the chat room. Both seemed strangely cold towards her from the start. At first she noticed that they both typed at the same odd staccato speed, but never at the same time as each other. Then she noticed they both misspelt certain words – as Dan did – until she was sure they were all the same person. Carol kept quiet. She didn't want people to feel that she was becoming paranoid. She'd already mentioned to one of the girls that Dan wasn't quite himself these days, but her remark was rudely brushed off.

Over a few days, Carol began to sense that the atmosphere in the chat room was definitely chilly towards her, even when Dan wasn't around. She couldn't put her finger on it, but it began to upset her. And then she made a shocking discovery.

One day, she was idly googling her name when she came across a website she hadn't seen in the search results before. Curious, she clicked on the link and then reeled back in shock. Looking at the images that unfolded, she felt wave upon wave of nausea, until she raced to the toilet, vomiting and heaving until there was nothing left. Creeping back to her computer, she stared at the screen. It was full of huge, grossly fat, naked bodies. And staring out from the folds of obscene flesh, over and over again, was her face. It had been photo-manipulated onto massive bodies. It was the most disgusting thing Carol had ever seen. The bodies were contorted to show their most intimate details full on to the viewer. Her name was plastered all over the site, along with disparaging remarks like, 'Pig,' 'Great White Whale,' and 'Cock Teaser'. Shaking, she turned off the machine. Instinctively she knew it. This had to be Dan.

The following morning, Carol called me. After showing Pete the website and explaining her suspicions to him, she'd called the police. They were sympathetic, and, yes, they could probably do something. However, for the time being resources were scarce, and these sorts of complaints were becoming more common. Unfortunately, her case would have to join a long queue before anything could be done.

Carol didn't want to wait. Her confidence was being severely undermined. What if someone she knew stumbled across the site? What if her children saw it? Her husband agreed. Fortunately he was completely understanding about the circumstances. He knew how much Carol loved her chat room people, and wasn't surprised to hear that she'd been supportive of Dan when his marriage fell apart. That's the sort of person she was.

In this case, it didn't take our IT people long to track down the owner of the site, and Dan got a surprise when he was served with legal papers to remove the content from the site immediately, and to desist from any further activities that were defamatory. And then the truth began to emerge. As the chat room social group began to hear of Dan's creative web work, they told Carol all about his campaign to turn them against her. He'd quietly suggested to them that Carol had come on to him, proposing a meeting for sex in Brisbane. They had been shocked. This wasn't the sort of chat room for that. They'd known each other for a long time, in some cases years. Dan had kept up the whispers, introducing two new phoney people to the chat room as everyone began to freeze Carol out. If he'd left it at that, Carol would have no doubt eventually left. But Dan's anger at his perceived rejection needed something more than an insidious and unfair campaign. He needed to express his bitterness by demeaning and ridiculing her publicly. But it was one step way too far.

Dan's days were numbered. Within a day or two, he was banned from all chat rooms hosted on that website. His IP address was also blacklisted. Alienated from his chat room friends, he was right out of his comfort zone, and had to find new playgrounds, build new relationships, and this time, hopefully, choose his words carefully.

Dan got out of that situation very lightly. It was fortunate for him that Carol decided not to sue him for defamation.

Defamation and the publishing of libellous material can have serious financial consequences for the publisher (Dan), and Carol certainly wouldn't have had a problem proving defamation in this case.

Lucky Break

'He had a vitamin deficiency'

My partner, Chris, and I had just started an eight hour shift and, straight up, had been allocated a job to attend a break and enter. We set out in the police car. On the way, I saw a cardboard box about the size of a small microwave oven sitting on the side of road at an intersection. I had no idea what was in it, but from the moment I saw it, that box really fascinated me. Luckily, Chris was driving, so, as we cruised past, I wound my window down and leaned out a bit to try to see what was inside.

I saw something black inside. That really got me going, but we were on our way to a job and didn't have time to stop and check it out. As we moved away, I'd already made up my mind to go back later.

At the scene of the break and enter, we interviewed the complainant and took the details for a crime report. I then asked Chris to take me back to the intersection where I'd seen the box. He was happy to do that but, just as the mysterious box came into sight, we received a code two job. This immediately took priority as code two meant we had to attend a situation urgently – a lights and sirens job.

As we flew past the box, I noticed a couple of kids standing next to it, looking in and kicking it around. I still couldn't see what was inside, and it was driving me mad. I had to pinch myself to get my mind back onto directing Chris to our assigned job.

It was a good two hours before we were back at the police station to wrap up the morning's paperwork. But that box kept popping into my head. I have a really inquisitive mind that won't let go of something intriguing until I have an answer for it. Finally I turned to my partner.

'I want to head over to check out that box,' I told him.

'What box?' he said, looking completely mystified.

'The one I mentioned when we passed it earlier today.'

'Oh, let it go,' he said. 'It's probably gone by now anyway. It was only a box.'

'Well, I'm going out on my own then.'

With that, I left Chris writing up some notes and hopped into the police car. This time I would find out what that bloody box was all about. Well, almost.

On the way, I came across two guys who appeared to be dancing on the footpath. As I drew closer, I saw that the situation was a bit more serious. They were, in fact, swinging punches at each other in a full-on fight. They were so into it that I had to put the flashing lights on and hit the siren a couple of times to get their attention. When I jumped out of the car and went over, I kept my distance. They were both as mad as hell, and just as likely to turn on me.

The next fifteen minutes was well spent calming those boys down. Gradually they began discussing their differences sensibly, and made up. Happily neither wanted to lay any charges, so I was soon free to return to the very pressing matter of that box.

I couldn't believe it. The box had gone. As I got out of the car to look around, I was suddenly so unreasonably disappointed that I had to shake myself. Was it really that important? But no, I still needed to solve the mystery. Where had the box gone? There was nothing in sight, so I took a drive around the nearby streets, just in case.

And then, right around a corner, there it was, tipped on its side. As I walked towards it, I could hear a scratching sound, and saw a lump of black feathers poking in and out. What the hell was it?

I bent to look inside, and found a very sick looking crow staring back at me. Now I love animals, and this poor thing was obviously suffering, so my first thought was to try to pick it up. But the crow wasn't having any of it. It must have been a sight. A uniformed police officer, hanging on to a large, wildly flapping, madly squawking bird right in the middle of the street. The things we do.

Obviously the box was the best place for my new friend, and although it was falling apart I managed to get the box and bird into the front seat of the police car. Now I needed help. Normally, a job radioed into Police Communications has a code to identify the type of job. However, try as I might, I couldn't find a code that fitted my situation. I simply had to inform Communications that I'd found a sick crow, and requested the location of the nearest vet.

There was a long silence. Little did I know the guys in Communications were cracking up. They could hardly believe their ears. If I'd known, I would have been delighted to have made everyone's day, I'm sure. As it was, once the vet's information was relayed to me in a flat, serious voice that was obviously itching to burst out laughing, the hilarious (and totally anonymous) comments began to stream in from other units. And it's amazing how many funny references to crows can be made over a few hours, believe me! But it was all good-natured fun, and anyone who was the butt of humour one day, would be the one laughing the next. We all knew that.

The vet was a bit more sympathetic than my colleagues, promising to check the bird out and let me know the outcome when I called during my afternoon shift the following day.

And I was delighted with that outcome. Apparently my crow had a simple vitamin deficiency, easily treated by a shot and a good rest. It had recovered sufficiently to have been released before I got there. How had it had ended up in the cardboard box? Perhaps someone had seen it was sick and tried to care for it, or maybe it had been trapped by children intending to torment it. I'll never know, but when I heard that it had happily flown away, I was pleased.

However, the smile of satisfaction was quickly wiped from my face when the vet presented me with a rather large bill for his services. I made sure to keep that under my hat for a while.

It takes Two to Tango

'Where was all the money going?'

Relationships interest me as much as the next person. We're fascinated by them. What makes a good relationship work? Why do some diabolical liaisons manage to struggle on through thick and thin? Couples can appear to be poles apart in their personalities, interests, or choice of friends, and yet they stick together, seemingly happy.

I've known some couples put up with a lot from each other. For example, one partner may accept another's bad mannered, loutish behaviour, another may turn a blind eye to some regular sexual indiscretion, or yet another may be aware that a partner is involved in criminal activities and be prepared to ignore the obvious signs. So why do they stay together for so long? Or, perhaps the question should be, why didn't they do anything about it until it was too late?

Pam was very happy in the first five years of her marriage to Bruce, her chef husband. They had two beautiful children, both at school, and, thanks to a very healthy inheritance from her parents' estate, lived in a lovely home in one of Melbourne's trendy, bayside suburbs. Money from the inheritance had also gone to financing a small restaurant for Bruce, and it was working very well, most of the time.

As Bruce told her, trading patterns are difficult to anticipate in the hospitality game. Sometimes a slump in covers meant more wastage, higher staff wages, and less profit, even a loss here and there. Cash injections, he insisted, were necessary to keep even a decent restaurant afloat from time to time.

Slim and good looking in a fiftyish sort of way, Bruce neither drank nor smoked. He was enormously energetic, staving off the paunch that many chefs manage to acquire. As far as Pam was aware he had only one weakness, and that was the horses. His father had been a track enthusiast, passing on the thrill of the races to his son. Tragically, his father had gambled away everything the family had owned, until he'd died, destitute and alone, so Pam wasn't exactly keen to see her husband show any interest in betting. Bruce assured her that he knew the difference between a bit of fun and being addicted.

It wasn't until the restaurant began to lose money regularly that Pam realised there was a problem. She couldn't understand why there should be so many outstanding creditors when the restaurant was always very, very busy whenever she called in there. It was also getting excellent reviews and the bookings, from what the staff told her, were solid.

But Pam had other things on her mind to worry about before the restaurant. The kids were becoming involved in after-school activities. With Bruce at the restaurant, she was left to do the ferrying from one sports venue to another. Pam didn't mind and, anyway, who else was going to do it?

Occasionally Pam would notice larger than normal withdrawals from their bank account. Bruce was always taking a couple of hundred here and there, but this was more in the thousands. When she remembered to ask Bruce about it, he was always too busy to give her more than, 'I paid so-and-so,' or, 'you know, it was a really bad week.' Something inside Pam stopped her from pressing Bruce about the money. After all, it belonged to them both, and he did have a business to run.

However, over the course of a year the withdrawals became more frequent, and the amounts began to frighten her. The figures of ten, fifteen and twenty thousand began to appear more often. Bruce was impossible to pin down on the subject, skittering away on some urgent errand whenever she brought it up. At other times he was too tired to talk about business, or he had a splitting headache.

When Pam called me she was angry.

'I've just had one of the restaurant staff call to say that she hadn't been paid for a month. I'm sick of this. I want to know what Bruce is doing with all this money.'

Talking to Pam further, she told me that she was seriously thinking of leaving her marriage. She'd known all along there was a problem with Bruce's gambling but had stuck her head in the sand. Now, though, she could see money draining away fast, and wanted it stopped. She wanted to salvage something out of her marriage before there was nothing left.

'How much do you think he's spent on gambling?' I asked.

There was a significant pause.

'Lots. I've no idea. Does it matter?'

I explained to Pam that if she could show a spending pattern in Bruce's gambling it was possible to estimate how much had been drained from their assets. This would assist her when it came to the allocation of funds in any subsequent divorce proceedings. It appeared, despite Bruce's efforts, that there were still considerable assets remaining in their joint names and Pam, if she could prove Bruce's excessive spending on the races, would be entitled to a greater share of those assets.

We would have to conduct a three month surveillance operation on Bruce to show a reasonable estimate of his gambling expenditure over time. This would be difficult, but, with a preliminary observation, we knew that he used the TAB a few doors down from his restaurant, and that helped enormously. We just needed eyes inside that TAB.

I brought Bookie Bill into the game. Bill knows more about horses than anyone I know. And he should, after spending fifty years of his life at the tracks. He was perfect for this sort of work, feeling utterly at home at the TAB. He's pleasant, affable to all, and extremely knowledgeable.

And his experience was a godsend. He could spend the entire day in the TAB, betting regularly with small amounts, and turning a moderate cheerful profit at close of business. He made sure that he didn't get too lucky, on some days taking an appropriate loss here and there with wry, good humour. In no time, both his fellow punters and the management loved Bill, making it easy for him to keep an eye on what was happening.

And it was all action. Bruce was a whirling dervish when it came to mixing work with pleasure. He would be one of the first customers of the morning, tearing through the door and placing his bets in a frenzied rush. That's when Bill saw a transformation in Bruce's behaviour. He'd be agitated and sweating heavily as he queued to place his bets, and then become relaxed, almost euphoric, as soon as the bets were placed. He'd almost float away from the TAB, heading back to the restaurant. Then, sometimes, in less than half an hour, he'd be back, eyes anxiously scanning his racing forms, clearly back on edge.

Bill was very careful not to suggest any advice or proffer any tips to anyone in the TAB just in case it influenced the direction or intensity of Bruce's betting. He needn't have worried. Bruce was on his own frantic agenda, only acknowledging Bill with a nod or two as he became familiar with my agent's presence. This made it much easier for Bill to keep a record of Bruce's expenditure and occasional winnings. It also wasn't long before informal chats with staff members were confirming most of his own observations.

Bruce had a serious addiction. Placing a bet was like getting a fix or taking a drug, giving a temporary state of ecstasy. However, the pleasure was short-lived and only fuelled the need for another hit. How he managed to run a successful, busy business and spend so much time betting was a masterpiece of time management. His mind must have been working overtime, juggling the day-to-day running of the restaurant with studying the form and racing information he needed to place his bets.

But Bruce was losing, and not just thousands of dollars a week, he was losing his wife, his home, and probably his children. Even the restaurant was going to be part of the frightening settlement he was about to face.

The question, of course, is could this problem have been nipped in the bud? With Pam's more positive intervention at an earlier stage, might Bruce have acknowledged and addressed his addiction? Or could Pam have arranged things so that the funds were not so easily accessible? There are wonderful resources out there such as Lifeline Australia and Gamblers Anonymous. If Bruce had been encouraged to face his problem in its early stages, and seek help, would he have ended up losing everything? We will never know.

Indecent Assault

'You won't be able to have children.'

It was Valentine's Day. I'd arrested a guy for drink driving and taken him to the Brisbane City Watchhouse to be charged in the usual way.

Once I'd filled out all the forms and checked the prisoner in, I waited while some of the paperwork was processed. That's when I saw a female prisoner being led out of a cell and escorted to the front desk, an area where charges[7] are read out by the desk sergeant.

I could see by her face and body language that she wasn't in a good mood, probably still affected by alcohol, or drugs, or both. Suddenly she went ballistic, swearing and screaming at the desk sergeant and other officers standing close by. As I watched, the situation escalated really quickly. She began

---

[7] This process ensures that prisoners acknowledge that they understand why they've been arrested so that they can be released to attend court at a later date.

to pick up anything she could lay her hands on and throw it around the room.

There must have been at least four officers moving in to restrain her at this point, but she was up for a real fight. She began swinging her fists at anyone who got close and became wild with anger. It wasn't a normal temper tantrum, it was if she was possessed – eyes bulging, face contorted – the works – as she tried to punch, kick and bite anything near her.

I stood well back against the wall. There were enough officers there to handle the woman, and any more would definitely have been in the way. Finally, the officers managed to pick her up and started to carry her to the padded cell. There she could go as crazy as she liked without hurting herself or anyone else.

As they carried her away from the front desk and passed close to me, she managed to get one of her legs loose. And just as I was noticing that she was wearing really chunky, wedge heeled shoes, she swung her leg straight at me, slamming her foot into my groin with incredible force. The kick was so hard that I was later told it lifted me about five centimetres off the ground before I crashed to the floor on my backside.

As the woman was carried to the padded cell, I was left writhing in absolute agony. I could feel wetness between my legs, which I later discovered was blood. I could hardly stand, so I asked Pete, my partner, to take me to hospital, where the doctor sent me straight in for an ultrasound because I was bleeding quite hard and had severe bruising to the groin area.

I laid in pain on a hospital bed waiting for a doctor to perform the ultrasound. When he arrived, looking very professional in his white coat, he didn't say a word, just slapped his cold instrument against my pelvic area and began his examination. I waited with bated breath, checking his eyes for some sign of a diagnosis, but they were totally expressionless. He didn't seem to register that I was a living human being. I felt so alone and afraid.

Suddenly he was finished.

'Your cervix has been damaged. You probably won't be able to have children,' he said, abruptly.

And that was it. Straight to the point with one of the most devastating pieces of news a young woman could be given, delivered without an inkling of sympathy or understanding. I had yet to meet my future husband, and here I was, being told that my chances of having children were extremely slim. As I began to cry, I was hardly aware of being booked in for an urgent laparoscopy[8].

Two days later, the laparoscopy was done and I was sent home to recover. Although I was on serious painkillers for

---

8   Laparoscopy (or peritoneoscopy) is a medical procedure used to examine the interior of the abdominal or pelvic cavities for the diagnosis or treatment (or both) of a number of different diseases and conditions. Source – www.betterhealth.vic.gov.au

days, I still couldn't believe the pain I was in. And that's me, a woman with a very high pain threshold.

But the pain was nothing compared to the gut wrenching disappointment I felt two days later when I went back to the hospital for my results. The doctor's voice echoed in my brain for months and months.

'Due to the extent of the kick you received to your pelvic area, your cervix was damaged. Your chances of having children are now limited.'

I left the doctor's office feeling empty and hollow. I had lost something I hadn't even had – children.

It was small consolation that the woman was later found guilty of serious assault resulting in my injuries, and dealt with at court. But the big break came a few years later when I became pregnant. Now I have two beautiful little girls, who I love with all my heart.

The Boss from Hell

'Your wife is a whore'

We're all unique individuals, but we have certain traits that are fairly common to us all. We are basically social animals, even the most reticent of us. After all, most of us spend our days among teeming communities of people, often shoulder to shoulder, as we shop, travel, work and play. So, most of the time, it's in our best interest to get on with everyone. But how often do we snarl at the checkout kids at our local supermarket? Oops, did I hit a bit of a nerve there? But, later, most of us feel like crap if we think we've upset a young person who is only trying to do their job to the best of their ability, don't we? But, of course, there's always the exception.

Chantelle has a high profile job in one of Sydney's top real estate companies. The company deals exclusively with multi-million dollar properties, most of which are traded through international markets. It's a very tough game, made harder by recent global economic woes and a softening of the real estate market in general.

But the financial ups and downs of other people don't trouble Chantelle in the least. She knows that there's still plenty of business out there, and, as far as she's concerned, that business is hers.

For the last seven years, Chantelle has gouged a reputation as one of the most ruthless individuals in an industry not normally known for its sensitivities. Known as The Fang by colleagues and competitors, she regards any high priced property as her domain alone, despite the involvement of any other agent or company. And she will do absolutely anything to get it into her portfolio, regardless of ethics, legalities, or moral considerations.

And, to make matters more unpalatable for her many detractors, she is undeniably beautiful. Lustrous raven hair surrounds an almost pixyish face, dominated by enormous, beguiling eyes that instantly mesmerise anyone unfortunate enough to be drawn into their range. Combining looks with an immaculate wardrobe and a perfect, catwalk figure, her presence in a room is both electrifying, and fearsome.

First thing in the morning, Chantelle walks from her high-end Mercedes, parked on the no-stopping lines outside the office. On her way past reception, and without a word, she tosses her car keys in front of the receptionist, who scrambles to move the vehicle around the back into Chantelle's private car park. The receptionist knows only one thing. If the vehicle gets a parking ticket, is towed, or is damaged in any way, The Fang will fire her.

Chantelle's progress through the open plan office to her own luxurious suite is a nightmare for the staff, as she slams her files onto desks, each covered in her frantic, barely legible scrawl. She berates and bullies as she goes through the work stations in her morning's line of fire.

'Are you totally incompetent, or do you just look that way?'

'Your nails are a disgrace. Don't touch any of my work until you've tidied them up.'

'How long does it take to do a search? Don't answer, I know you don't know.'

'How long have you worked here? Five minutes by the looks of this.'

'You idiot, are you writing copy, or copying copy from some other moron?'

Eventually the door to her suite slams shut, leaving the staff totally demoralised. There is never a single hint of praise or acknowledgement of work well done. Every encounter is an emotional holocaust of derision and criticism.

Not surprisingly, staff turnover is extremely high and, for Don, the principal of the business, that's an ongoing trial. Loyal, competent, and well experienced personnel are easily reduced to tears after a Fang tirade, and are often more than ready to resign. But Don, ever the pragmatist, knows who is bringing the really big money into the business. And even after Chantelle extracts her horrendous commission from him, it's her sales that are keeping the place afloat. So, what can he do? The last time he took Chantelle to one side and appealed to her sensitivities, she told him to 'grow some balls'.

At the other end of the spectrum entirely is Carl, her financier husband. Their relationship is a constant source of wonderment to all who know them. Slightly built and balding, Carl walks around with an expression of slight bewilderment that belies a powerful intellect and an uncanny business sense. But it's his quietly spoken pleasant nature – a total contrast to Chantelle's complete bitchiness – that gets people questioning. And since Chantelle never deigns to set foot in the coffee room, that's where people really let loose.

'But he's such a lovely, gentle person!'

'How does she talk to him at home?'

'How can he stand her, poor bastard?'

'Maybe he likes those designer heels stomping all over his backside.'

At regular intervals, Chantelle throws open her door, glares around the office, and heads for one of her frequent appointments. Fortunately, most of these are scheduled, so her Benz is ready and waiting for her at the front door. However she sometimes takes everyone by surprise, including her two PAs, by arriving at reception unexpectedly, and waiting, foot tapping impatiently, while someone rushes to retrieve her car.

On one particular morning, shortly after she'd reduced Del, one of the young researchers, to tears for the second time that week, she swirled around the corner into reception with her head in her Blackberry. Unfortunately, Del was coming in the other direction and, in the collision, Chantelle's Blackberry skittered to the floor. A horrifying silence ensued as Del cowered against the wall and the receptionist looked on with a mixture of fear and sympathy. Del had only been with the company for six months, and it looked like she wouldn't be making it to her seventh.

'Pick the fucking thing up, you stupid little bitch.'

Mortified with embarrassment, Del dropped to her knees and crawled over to the device. It looked undamaged, the screen still lit with a message. Through her welling tears she could see the words – Usual room, missed you. D.

Del sobbed in relief and scrambled to her feet. She'd snagged her tights on the polished timber floor – great. Holding out the Blackberry, she averted her eyes from Chantelle's vicious gaze. The device was snatched from her hand, and, when she looked up, Chantelle was gone. Moments later, the receptionist hurried back to her desk after delivering Chantelle's car. Her expression was anxious, and the news wasn't good.

'Sorry, Del. She says that's the last straw. You have to go at the end of the week.'

Del had just moved in to share a unit with her boyfriend, Stuart, who had lost his job with an IT company through downsizing only the previous week. What a disastrous situation! She had managed to stay clear of Chantelle's fury until two days ago, and then got hit twice on the same day. On both occasions, she'd been given papers to prepare that were way beyond her training and competency. Thanks to The Fang's regular attacks, there were staff shortages, so Del accepted the work, thinking she could help out. It had taken a lot of time to research the information, and she'd stayed back at the office until late to complete it. One of the more experienced girls had taken a look at her efforts and told her it was a job well done, but clearly The Fang had a different opinion.

Anyway, that was yesterday, and now, today, the Blackberry incident added up to three strikes, and that was more than enough for Chantelle. Del considered appealing to Don, but she knew it was pointless. When Chantelle fired someone, they stayed fired. Don was gutless where The Fang was concerned.

Morosely, Del plodded through her work, accepting sympathetic nods and occasional kind words from the other staff. Despite The Fang's monstrous influence, they were a great team. From time to time, Del's imagination soared with acts of revenge before coming down to earth with the sure knowledge she was out of her league. But then, as she checked her phone for messages, an image of The Fang's Blackberry screen flashed into her mind. She remembered the words – Usual room, missed you. D. They meant absolutely nothing to Del, but what if they could be made to mean something to, say, The Fang's husband? It was a very poor consolation prize, but Del could at least stir up a little bit of trouble for that evil woman. All she needed was The Fang's husband's email address. And she knew who could get it for her.

At 9.30 that night, Stuart was sitting at her console, tapping enthusiastically.

'Why did they give everyone all these access codes?' he asked, amazed at the vulnerability of the system.

'Oh, when I started, someone said that the email is so dodgy that we need them for a workaround, something like that,' Del told him, sipping her tea. 'Apparently, for all the money the company makes, Don is still a tight bum when it comes to technology. Just look at all these crappy monitors, and this is supposed to be a classy outfit!'

'OK,' Stuart said, sitting back for a moment. 'What do you want to say here?'

It was Carl, Chantelle's husband, who called me, and he seemed unnaturally calm as he explained the situation. He'd received a private email around midmorning the previous day from Don, the principal of the real estate company his wife worked for. Carl was surprised, because the rare emails between the two of them in the past had been through his business address. Carl's private email was for friends and family only.

The message was brief. 'Your wife is a whore. Ask her where she was on Tuesday at 2pm, and who she was with.'

'I called Don straight away. I've known the man for twenty years, and never known him use language like that.'

'What did he say?' I asked.

'He was enraged, to be frank, hysterical almost, and not a little afraid, I would suppose. My wife is, shall we say, a difficult woman.'

'So, do you know who sent the email?'

'No, not at this point. Don thinks it's a disgruntled staff member, and, god knows, there'll be enough of those in that place.'

'But to have the email sent from Don's email address or computer needs some technical know-how. Have his IT people had a look?'

'No. We decided it would be better to ignore it unless there's a repetition. The fallout in the company would be enormous should my wife find out someone's throwing mud her way. I mean she's really not an easy person to get on with.'

I was lost for words. Carl had just told me that they weren't doing anything about the situation. So why was he calling me?

'What can I do for you?' I asked.

'Ah, yes, what I'd like you to do is find out if it's true.'

The penny dropped.

'The only problem,' Carl continued, 'is that my wife is a fast moving storm. I think even the very best investigator would find it extremely difficult to keep up with her.'

'Perhaps we can use DNA for a fairly quick result,' I suggested. 'Unless you want to know who it is.'

Carl laughed pleasantly. 'That's assuming there is a 'who' here.'

This guy was amazing. Here we were discussing his wife's possible infidelity and he was as calm and charming as if we were just having a lovely social chat.

'We can determine the presence of seminal fluid from a person's underwear,' I suggested.

'Mmm, that's a problem. She doesn't wear any. Says it spoils the line of her clothes. How about a tampon?'

'That's different,' I said, a little surprised, 'however many women do avoid sexual intercourse during menstrual flow, so it does cut down our chances. Is it possible to get hold of one of her skirts or trousers, maybe something that has a dried stain on it?'

'That's easy,' he said. 'I'm the dry cleaning wallah in the house. I drop everything off on my way to the office. I can easily slip you a couple of things. She's not into wearing the same thing for weeks, if ever again. So how does it work?'

I explained that we'd test the stains for the presence of semen, and, if it showed positive, send it for DNA profiling. We would also need a sample of saliva for his DNA profile too. In that way we could eliminate him from the results.

Carl chuckled. He really was cool about all this.

'That's easy. How reliable are the results? I mean, are you ever wrong?'

'We always say 99.99% certain,' I told him. 'We have to allow for coincidences ...'

'Like people getting something off a toilet seat, you mean?' he said, laughing.

'No,' I said. 'As you know, that doesn't wash anymore. It used to be an excuse for getting a sexually transmitted disease, but we know better these days.'

Two weeks later, the real estate office was set buzzing as two security officers walked into the building and went into Don's office. After ten minutes, they emerged with Don and went into Chantelle's suite. Her screams of rage, and foul invective went on for a full five minutes and could be heard throughout the entire building.

Eventually she appeared, shaking off a security officer who was holding her arm.

'You pack of fucking wankers, all of you. You poor pathetic creatures. My husband owns this dump, and I'll make sure you're all looking for jobs tomorrow, believe me.'

There was a moment of silence before one of the girls in the main office rose to her feet and began a slow handclap. Laughter rustled through the room as, one after another, the entire staff stood and joined the clapping. Chantelle scowled, striding towards reception. But the receptionist beat her to it.

Meeting Chantelle halfway across the office, she tossed her car keys onto an unoccupied desk and walked away.

Carl called to thank me for the prompt work.

'You know,' he remarked conversationally, 'I bought into Don's business to keep Chantelle busy and out of trouble, never realising how much heartache she caused. Oh, I know she had problems communicating from time to time, we all do. But when Don gave me the low-down I was shocked. She would come home at night with flowers and tell me the staff had given them to her. And the poor bloke felt he couldn't do anything. I've left my money in there, but I'm appointing a manager to make sure the staff is treated fairly in future, including those I've asked to be reinstated. With Chantelle out of the picture, they'll soon all be selling well.'

'I'm glad the tests were negative,' I said, meaning it. Carl seemed like a really nice guy.

'Yes, I didn't really doubt it. She's not in the least bit interested in sex, and never has been. Maybe a lover would do her some good. At least this exposed the real problem. They called her The Fang, can you imagine that?'

Better Than the Real Thing

'Hey, don't I know you?'

Normally I'm a jeans and T shirt sort of person. That's how I get around the office. I want to be cool and comfortable while I multitask: on the phone to clients and agents (sometimes simultaneously), searching our on-line data banks, downloading voice and video recordings, remembering to drink my coffee, and even ready to jump into a vehicle and relieve an agent on a surveillance job that's unexpectedly gone from four to fourteen hours in duration. We're busy, really busy, and that's what makes this work so worthwhile, that, and knowing that the next call could be from someone who desperately needs our help.

So I guess clothing and fashions don't really interest me unless it's part of the job, and then watch out! When it comes to using clothing and accessories as part of changing my persona, I'm in my element. That's when the glamour of being a spy creeps into my psyche. And most women I've met are much the same. There's a thrill of excitement when we contemplate changing our appearance for some covert action. Walking into a hotel, dressed and made up to make heads turn, is powerful, and when you know that nobody is about to recognise you, it's beyond your wildest dreams.

Of course some of the work is down and dirty. In the early days I had my share of grubby shorts, stained T shirt, and hair a sweaty mess, as I worked in the stinking heat posing as a gardener across from my target's house. Who wants more of that?

And there are moments of victory to remember. One target was proving extremely difficult to serve documents on. He worked in an office and was being protected by his colleagues, so it was impossible for my agent to get to him personally. Eventually, fed up with the delays, I dressed in the most provocative outfit I could conjure without being arrested for indecent exposure. I use the term 'dressed' lightly, as everything was hanging out.

We already knew the sort of female our target found attractive, so I was the ultimate bimbo when I sashayed up to the reception desk and asked for him. Tony wasn't there, of course, but by the time all the guys had come to the foyer to get an eyeful, he was beginning to wish he was.

I told the receptionist that I'd wait for him at the coffee shop across the road. And, sure enough, Tony couldn't help himself, swaggering in five minutes later. He got a terrible shock when I told him he was served, and handed him the documents. And then he became angry, telling me 'that doing things that way is unfair'. Really?

Some time ago, to have a little rest from investigating infidelity, I took some work tracking counterfeit goods. This was retail therapy on steroids. Imagine, you are given an open brief to shop and, in the process, discover if a retailer is trading in counterfeit handbags, shoes, perfumes, and clothing. It was an awful task, spending time visiting Australia's shops and markets, sifting through a wonderful array of fashion and accessories.

Sometimes the retailer would infer, or even admit, that the goods weren't the real deal. By and large the retailers were lovely, basically good folk, just trying to make a living. My job was to buy the questionable item and send it to the company that supposedly manufactured the designer label, and wait for their verdict. The wait was never long, and the pronouncement was always 'fake'. I would then revisit the retailer with a statement for them to sign declaring that they would cease selling the item. This was always a shock for them because they didn't expect things to be done that way. I guess they imagined that, if it ever happened, there would be uniforms and arrests. I felt sorry for some of them. I know that a few had stockpiles of goods they would be stuck with, unless they tried to sell them somewhere else. But the genuine brand companies lose millions of dollars a year through trading in counterfeit goods.

They have to protect their brand, and, in doing it this way, at least they're giving offenders the chance to stop. And there's another issue. Counterfeit goods are often produced in illegal sweat shops where children as young as five are locked up for twelve hour shifts. The children are trapped in squalid dormitories, poorly fed, and badly clothed.

A few weeks later I would come back to check that the retailer was adhering to the agreement to desist. That's when I had to be careful. I couldn't afford to be recognised because the word would quickly get around and the phoney gear would disappear off the shelves and stalls in a flash before I could get to them. In a large market, an operator could have ten stalls, all worked by family members and friends, and all on high alert.

I would have to regularly consult my wardrobe – every woman's dream, I suppose. And I've noticed something quite interesting about this. When I dress in different outfits, my personality changes according to what I'm wearing. It just happens, I'm aware of it, and it's extremely useful. For instance, when I dressed like a bimbo for that guy I served the papers on, I behaved like a bit of a slut with his co-workers when they came out to ogle. It was easy, it was a persona I slipped into, and knowing that I was blindsiding them helped me to push the boundaries close to outrageousness. I was leading them by their noses, and I have to admit that it was fun.

When I want to be confident and feel respected, I power dress. The no-nonsense corporate business woman in me comes out to play. Smart business wear lifts my game automatically. It forces me to speak intelligently, to think before I say anything, and to become more calculated in my conversations. But that won't necessarily work for me if I'm gathering information. Smartly dressed, self-assured women are perceived to know the kind of information I'm looking for, so if I'm asking questions that don't fit my image, you can bet someone's brain goes 'tick, tick, tick, something wrong here'. So I have to become the bubbly, easily impressed blonde asking, 'Ooh, is that how it works? You guys are so amazing.'

And do I make mistakes? Yes, of course I do. Once, instead of checking my notes on a particular counterfeit case, I relied on my memory and went to a market dressed in the same outfit that I'd worn on a previous occasion. Back then, the stallholder had been pleasant though extremely nervous, sweating heavily when I'd presented him with the agreement to desist selling fake designer shoes. This was my follow-up visit to make sure he was behaving himself. The stall was chocker with phoney gear. He'd even moved into handbags and purses. Surprised at his audacity, I began to take photos. The stallholder, a thick-set, big bellied man, recognised me and lost the plot completely. Despite his size, he was around to the front of his stall in an instant, grabbing me by the throat, spitting and jabbering into my face.

I was lucky. There were enough men around to take offence at this huge bloke strangling a little blonde girl, so they dragged him off. That taught me a sharp lesson – never take an operation for granted. Anything can happen, absolutely anything.

The longer I work in this field, the more I have to take care that I'm not recognised. I don't do so much of the field work these days, except in special, complex cases. I have agents to manage, and administration work that is demanding enough. But I am still sometimes recognised from past undercover operations, although it's usually more a double-take than being precisely identified. I see that 'where do I know you from' look in their faces. And anyway, who'd be keen to start a conversation in the local bakery with, 'Hey, didn't you have a drink with me one night?' after being caught out cheating on his wife.

There's a lot of romanticism attached to working in disguise. But most ordinary people aren't aware of being followed, even if they're doing something naughty, so we don't often wear false eyebrows and moustaches, wigs, loads of different hats, and those sorts of things. A change of clothing style is enough to do the trick, along with some glasses. It's funny when I see my target look around and actually look right through me. The unconscious part of the brain has dismissed me as being totally innocuous. It's the crims who're extremely observant and hyper-vigilant but, like everyone else, they can be dumb too. They're more likely to know they are under surveillance and yet they'll leave their mobile phones somewhere stupid, meet someone they shouldn't, or give away something critical in a phone conversation. Thank goodness we're all human, because it makes my job so much easier.

Smash and Grab

'He's hiding in the back of the shop'

One night, during a late evening general duties shift, I was working with my partner, Garry, when we had a call to a break and enter at a bicycle shop. Apparently a car had been driven through the shop window, and both the vehicle and the driver were still inside the building.

As we arrived, lights blazing and sirens screaming, I jumped out of the police vehicle and ran over to a sedan parked halfway through the front of the shop to check that no-one was injured inside it. The shop itself was in darkness, so I couldn't see in at all well, just making out the outlines of a few bikes lined up for sale.

By that time, another couple of patrol cars had arrived, so we all stood at the shop front discussing what we should do. With all the excitement, adrenalin was running and we were all on edge. A check of the shop's rear window and door showed that there'd been no forced exit through the back, so there was a strong feeling that the driver could be hiding somewhere at the back of the shop.

We knew one of us would have to enter the shop to see if the suspect was still inside. But we knew nothing about him. He could be totally whacked out on drugs, or heavily armed. We had no idea. Of course, I drew the short straw and was volunteered to check the shop out with my torch.

Climbing over the front of the crashed vehicle, I crept into the shop. I needn't have bothered. The floor was littered with broken glass that crunched under my feet however carefully I went. I kept thinking that they could hear me, but I couldn't hear them. I also knew that their eyes would have had time to adjust to the darkness, and mine hadn't, making it too easy for them to jump out and grab me.

My mag light gave me a path of light towards the rear of the shop where the staff room was. A quick scan of the showroom had revealed nothing but rows of bicycles, all gleaming in different colours. There was no other choice, I had to go right to the back, and so, taking a deep breath, I went towards the staff room.

As I walked closer to the back, my mind was running wild. I imagined some crazed lunatic hiding there with a gun, ready to shoot me. Or some man with a knife ready to stab me as soon as I walked around the corner. Breaking into a cold, clammy sweat, I realised that I had to try to control my thinking and remain calm. My nervous anticipation was scaring the crap out of me.

I took one last look at my colleagues staring back at me from outside the shop, giving me gestures of support and encouragement. I knew where they preferred to be. My heart pounding in my chest, I took another deep breath, and stepped into the staff room.

My scream of fright must have been heard blocks away.

'Help! Help! He's here!' I yelled, fumbling for my baton.

As officers thundered through the shop to provide backup, I realised my mistake. My dangerous suspect, unmoving and staring right back at me, was simply a store dummy dressed in cycling gear.

I had to endure my co-workers retelling that story for many months, and it never fails to draw a smile whenever I think of it now.

Tools of the Trade

'My top selling item is a mini voice recorder'

Walking into one of Australia's spy shops isn't quite the romantically covert experience you might imagine. I've heard people express surprise that such places exist and, when asked what they envisage, find they commonly expect something out of a John le Carré novel.

Sadly there are no seedy looking characters with thick foreign accents lurking in dark corners, hunched over suspicious tangles of wires, peering up myopically whenever the ancient doorbell jangles. Instead, casual visitors will inevitably find themselves in a well lit showroom, faced with an array of glass cabinets displaying a fascinating range of electronic gadgetry.

Surveillance or counter surveillance? That is one question. Do I want to listen in on someone's conversation, or discover whether I'm being bugged?

Where is the surveillance to take place – in a vehicle, on a computer, in an office, or at home? Once some of these questions are answered, the product I'm looking for becomes more easily defined.

If I'm intending to set up video surveillance in a room, I have to decide whether a short term observation with a nanny cam hidden in the bottom of a bag will do the trick. If a longer surveillance is required, I need to decide between a cam installed in a piece of furniture, an ornament, a wall or in the ceiling. And do I want the cam to transmit to a computer nearby, or record to a storage device?

Soon my choices are narrowed down by my requirements and the operational circumstances, and whether I'm listening, watching, or both, I can buy what I need for the job. And there's plenty of gadgetry left over for the wannabe spy.

Of course I can't discuss how the private investigation industry uses surveillance equipment. I do still have to meet agents in dark alleys and seedy clubs, so I'm not about to give away any trade secrets. I'm joking, of course, about the dark alleys at least. But let's take a tongue-in-cheek look at some of the gear that's readily available in an Australian spy shop.

The Button Cam

This is a wireless device consisting of a high resolution camera disguised to look like a normal button. The button is worn on the outside of an item of clothing, while the attached transmitter and receiver are concealed on the body. The button can make wearing haute couture a little challenging. Sometimes a button (cloth covered or otherwise) is difficult to accessorise, making life extremely complex for the fashionista. Luckily for men, the button can be substituted by a screw, so all the budding handymen out there can easily incorporate one into their tool belts. Off duty tradies can use the screw as a sort of lapel badge.

The Spy Pen

Certainly mightier than any sword its size, this tiny DVR is built into a ballpoint pen that records audio/video for up to three hours. The recording is downloaded to a PC where specific software is used to view it. And the pen actually works.

Of course there are obvious disadvantages to using these items. To start with, there are always pen thieves around (check out the pen holder cam later) and the dollars will mount up if you continually allow these pens to stray. There are also fiddlers and chewers. Some people can't help themselves when they're in a stressful environment. They unconsciously fiddle, causing pens to jump apart and disgorge springs and vital components everywhere. That can be embarrassing. And the chewers can really mess up the quality of a recording. Remember – surveillance and saliva don't mix.

The Spy Watch

The next time someone keeps shoving their wristwatch in your direction, it's not necessarily because they want to clock your admiration for their classy timepiece. There may be a lens hidden in the watch face, with two hours of battery power for audio/visual recording. The watch also doubles as a USB flash drive.

You can bet this little clever piece of work doesn't sport any designer labels. In fact, it looks so ordinary that the spy who favours the chunkier, macho dive watch may find this one just too pathetic for his hard nut image. It's amazing how many difficult decisions a spy has to make.

Spy Sunglasses

A must have for the budding spook. Supplied with an MP4 recorder with two hours recording on one charge, the pinhole camera captures colour audio/video. Now you know why so many people wear their sunnies indoors. They're all watching each other for fashion tips. You can always tell when a person is using spy sunglasses because they're intent on moving their heads slowly at all times to avoid motion blur. Sometimes they may also have a bad hangover.

A great deal of skill is also required to record correctly, particularly when the sunglasses are shoved up onto the head, or dangled under the chin. Of course, a frolic in the surf, in bed, or on water skis, becomes extremely hazardous to recording quality.

The Pen Holder Cam

This desk clock and pen holder looks innocuous enough, but hides a mini video camera that sends footage to a receiver in a VCR, DVR or TV. You can check out who's stealing your favourite pen. Laughing? This is actually an important issue. There are countless cases where office staff will steal from each other. In some workplaces nothing is sacred – lunches, booze, biscuits, coffee mugs, and, above all, pens. This device will faithfully record who took what as your office is stripped bare. That's unless the silly thing is stolen, of course.

The Alarm Clock Cam

A very cute, cheerful, little alarm clock, this one sends audio/video to a VCR, DVR or TV. Wake up time with a difference! This can bring home the shocking truth – you can finally catch that damn dog sleeping on the bed while you're at work. And if you're doing anything naughty yourself, make sure it's not activated. There's nothing worse than the kids watching while you ... Feeling guilty all of a sudden? You know you'll never look at your teddy bear alarm the same way again.

Mini Voice Recorder

This very popular item looks like a small USB stick and can be used as such. But with 1GB of storage, it can hold over sixty hours of voice recording. It's easy to see why this device is a big seller. Extremely small and portable, it can be easily concealed in a bra or wide armpit. In some cases, it could come in handy to record the questions that weren't asked because someone forgot to switch it on. Of course, when the memory is full, some lucky person does have to listen to all that chatter.

GPS Tracker

At around $500, you'd hate to see this one disappear across the Nullarbor in a cloud of dust. Identifying the location of a vehicle, person, or item of property within fifteen metres, and reporting back to a mobile phone in real time, this device is extremely versatile.

However, if a clever spy on the other side detects the tracker, it could lead to some interesting and expensive counter surveillance tactics. Just imagine super-spy spending seventeen days on the Trans Siberian Railway before discovering the tracker in a package on its way to Vladivostok.

Directional Long Range Listening Device

For the person who doesn't have a hundred-channel cable TV connection, this could be the perfect gift. They can find a home with a convenient TV broadcasting the program they want, and just sit outside the house and enjoy. There is a certain loss of control when you don't have access to the remote, but some householders would probably be amenable to program requests, and may even invite the listener in for a nice cup of tea.

And don't think you're immune from someone eavesdropping on you from the other side of the supermarket car park. You will need to carefully muffle your voice when discussing your latest tax lurk, because some devices will easily pick up conversations at 300 metres. Watch out for the man with the strange looking brolly.

VHF Line Transmitter

This is basically a phone tap, and is questionably legal. It transmits phone conversations from the line it's attached to from up to 100 metres away. This device can break just about every law under the sun, resulting in hundreds of years in the slammer. Be careful! In fact, don't even think about it.

Bug Detection Kits

And who is watching you? Perhaps you need a radio frequency detector, probe, and hidden camera detector so you can sleep easily at night. Unless the recording or transmitting devices have been installed by top-of-the-line professionals with extraordinary resources, these detection kits work quite well. It just takes a little time to do an effective sweep, which usually has a negative effect on foreplay.

The sweeps do have to be done frequently, which is a bit of a chore. Most criminals have gorillas to do that sort of work, but can they be trusted? Of course, you can always get the kids to do it for you, and you know they'll do a better job. For around $3,000, the kit's yours.

Voice Changing Phone

Wondered why all those overseas call centre folk sound different? They must have one of those phones designed to change a voice beyond recognition. Great for handling staff in a big PI agency – nobody will know who the boss really is.

Night Vision Headset

This is the absolute in headgear for the agent who wants to be taken seriously at the pub. The goggles come with a flip-up mask that is truly de rigueur. But can he see in the dark? Absolutely. The built in, high-powered IR illuminator, image intensifier tubes, and high light gain, will see to that, whatever that all means.

These are really handy in dimly lit nightclubs. Not only will everyone appreciate the fact that the wearer is an experienced agent, but it makes checking out the talent a lot easier. Kissing is quite another matter, and requires entirely different equipment.

Flexible Mini Spy Cam

Perfect for all those dark places, this little cam is attached to a flexible tube. It has an LED light so you can check mouse holes, tightly packed fridges, under your child's bed, in fact anywhere really difficult to get to. You could almost conduct your own colonoscopy.

USB Keylogger

This device, attached to the USB cable, records all the keystrokes from a computer keyboard, storing them for downloading later. This is very convenient for retrieving all those forgotten passwords, or finding out what your children are typing, although, if you're older than fifteen, you probably won't be able to understand what they're actually saying.

Spy Software

This is a downloadable stealth program to monitor computer activity such as sent and received emails, chats, visited websites, online searches, programs used, file transfers, and keystrokes. Just about everything that is done on a computer can be recorded remotely. And if this program has been installed on a naughty person's computer, they're completely sunk.

Not for Sale

Pop into most spy shops in the US, and you can also purchase powerful tasers, pepper sprays, telescopic steel batons (with or without the LED light), and, the ultimate, a 950,000 volt, knuckle duster stun gun. Ouch!

All investigation enquiries to:

Detection Group Pty Ltd
www.detectiongroup.com.au
enquiry@detectiongroup.com.au
1300 780 833

GPO Box 5091, Brisbane
Queensland 4001

Our Recommended Businesses:

Web & Graphic Design
Australdata
www.australdata.com

Michael Hessenthaler
michael@australdata.com.au

Business Cards, Design & Printing
Visual distraction
www.visualdistraction.com.au

Michael Reardon
create@visualdistraction.com.au

Chartered Accountants
AW Munro & Co
www.awmunro.com.au

Mark Burnham
info@awmunro.com.au

Book Printing
Self Publish Australia
www.selfpublish.com.au

Jason Swiney
jason@selfpublish.com.au

Banking
Bank of Queensland, Kenmore
www.boq.com.au

Monica Culey
monica.culey@boq.com.au
0402 107 597

Handyman Services
Ron Johnson
0416 144 333

Billboard Advertising
APN Outdoor
www.apnoutdoor.com.au

Jordan Clements
jordan.clements@apnoutdoor.com.au

Creative Writing
Dream Sight Corporation Pty Ltd
www.your-ghostwriter.com

Michael Collins & Jane Teresa Anderson
ghostwritermc@gmail.com

Public Relations
Profile PR
www.profilepr.net

Louise Van Ristell
louise@profilepr.net

kisspublications.com.au